THE
Pasta and Pizza
COOKBOOK
MYRA STREET

THE
Pasta and Pizza
COOKBOOK
MYRA STREET

Grange
BOOKS

A QUINTET BOOK

Published by Grange Books
An Imprint of Grange Books plc
The Grange
Grange Yard
London SE1 3AG

This edition published 1994

ISBN 1-85627-607-4

This book was designed and produced by
Quintet Publishing Limited
6 Blundell Street, London N7 9BH

Art Director: Peter Bridgewater
Editor: Nicholas Law
Photographer: John Heseltine

Typeset in Great Britain by
Context Typesetting, Brighton
Colour origination in Hong Kong by
Hong Kong Graphic Arts Company Limited, Hong Kong
Printed in China

CONTENTS

INTRODUCTION

PASTA

Pasta and pizza are two of Italy's best loved foods. Both are nutritious, fun to cook, interesting to eat and inexpensive. Use as many fresh ingredients as possible when preparing the toppings.

PASTA

Museum records in Italy suggest that pasta was being eaten in Rome during the 13th century and it is likely that it was eaten even earlier than this. The story of Marco Polo bringing noodles back from China in 1295 is widely told, but it seems likely that he did more for the spice trade than for pasta. The controversy as to whether it was the Chinese or the Italians who invented noodles will no doubt continue, as it has for centuries past.

Pasta is the Italian generic name for a dough made from flour and water. It is rolled thinly and cut into various shapes. The commercial variety is dried carefully to enable it to be stored for some time before use. Commercially produced pasta of the finest quality is made from the hard pure wheat known as 'durum' which is now grown mainly in Italy, North America, Russia and Canada. This hard durum wheat produces pasta which has a superior cooking quality and a better taste than that made with softer less expensive wheats. Always check on the packet before buying dried pasta that it is made with 100% durum wheat.

The Italians have elevated pasta to the status of a 'divine food' and their talent for using the finest fresh vegetables and herbs transforms simple pasta dishes into gourmet delights. There are probably different pasta shapes for every day of the year in Italy and there are certainly many different shapes widely available now. In the richer north of Italy, pasta is often made in flat noodle shapes with eggs; in the south it is more often made without eggs and is tubular in form. A discussion of the many shapes and names of all the different pastas would fill almost a separate book. For the purpose of the recipes in this book, I have kept to the better known shapes which are interchangeable in many recipes.

The popularity of this excellent and nutritious food has soared recently and there is now a wide variety of dried and fresh pasta available in supermarkets. Many specialist shops now make and sell fresh pasta.

Pasta is the perfect food for busy cooks. It needs no preparation unless you are making your own, cooks in minutes and is versatile enough to be eaten in soups, as an appetizer and as a main course.

HERBS

There is no doubt that fresh herbs have much to add to the flavours we create in the kitchen. As it is possible to buy potted herbs from garden centres and packets of fresh herbs from many supermarkets and vegetable shops, it is worth the effort to cook with fresh herbs.

Many of the herbs so characteristic of Italian cooking were originally used by the Romans medicinally as well as in the cooking pot. With the increasing interest in fresh food and healthy diets, most people are also more aware of the value and taste of fresh herbs. It is worth cultivating your own as they are decorative and edible. Many urban gardeners grow their own herbs very successfully, even on widow-sills and balconies and it is certainly interesting to try. Here are a few which grow in town most successfully and which are indispensable in pasta and pizza cooking. Dried herbs are inevitably necessary at certain times of the year and they make quite acceptable substitutes; it is best to buy them in small quantities as and when you need them. A jar of dried herbs which has been in the cupboard for over a year will not have much flavour.

BASIL

A wonderful aromatic herb which is decorative as well as useful. Basil is an excellent herb for flavouring tomato sauces to accompany pasta and an essential ingredient in the authentic Genoese pesto sauce.

Basil plants need sun and a warm sheltered position. Pinching the tops of the plants will encourage the plant to bush and prevent flowers growing. If you move it to the kitchen window-sill in winter, you should manage to keep a small supply of fresh basil going for a couple of months.

BAY

Bay trees are ideal for balconies and patios. The tree should be kept in a sheltered position in winter. When removing leaves for culinary use, take care not to spoil the shape. The occasional clipping of branches and constant picking of leaves will usually remove the need for heavy pruning. An essential ingredient in bouquet garni.

CHIVES

This spiky herb belonging to the onion family is excellent for flavouring sauces and dressings. It grows well in pots and can usually be divided after a couple of years if grown in good soil. It freezes well for use in the winter.

CORIANDER

This distinctive plant with dark green glossy leaves is one of the hardier southern European herbs. It is used extensively in oriental cookery and is good for flavouring vegetable dishes as well as making a pretty garnish. Coriander can be grown in pots or tubs.

DILL

This is another pretty culinary herb that can be grown in tubs or pots. Fresh dill goes particularly well with many fish dishes and sauces. The long feathery fronds also make a pretty garnish.

MARJORAM/ORIGANUM

The decorative wild marjoram is also easily grown in small containers and is suitable for flavouring sauces to accompany pasta. Its flavour is not quite as strong as that of the Mediterranean variety, origanum.

MINT

The many varieties of mint all have slightly different flavours. Experiment with two or three different mints until you find the ones you like best. The leaves are widely used in cooking. Mint leaves add taste and body to pasta salads and are also an attractive garnish. Two of the most popular varieties are apple mint and spearmint.

PARSLEY

Many varieties of parsley can be grown in large pots and tubs. Parsley can be used in quite large quantities and therefore it is cheaper to grow it from seed than to buy whole plants.

ROSEMARY

This is another plant discovered for the Western world by the Romans. It must be planted in a sheltered position to survive the winter in colder climates. Rosemary is a pretty, spiky bush and its aromatic leaves are a must for cooking, especially in lamb and vegetable dishes.

SAGE

A distinctive plant with silvery leaves which has the advantage of being fairly hardy once it is established. The leaves are particularly popular in savoury stuffings. This herb should be grown in a large pot and be left for a year before being robbed of too many leaves.

THYME

This is yet another plant which comes from the Mediterranean region. There are several pretty varieties which can be grown in pots and they all provide flavourings for many of the classic sauces which accompany pasta. The little spiky leaves are evergreen and can be picked and used even in the winter.

BOUQUET GARNI

This is a small bunch of fresh or dried herbs that are tied together with a piece of string. The string can be tied to the handle of a saucepan so that the whole bunch of herbs can be easily removed once it has imparted its flavour. Dried herbs are better placed in small muslin (cheesecloth) bags.

There are now many different commercially prepared bouquet garni sachets for sale which are good substitutes for fresh herbs that are not available. Quality herbalists still pack the herbs in muslin bags but the major commercial brands of bouquets garnis rather resemble teabags.

To make a fresh bouquet garni, take and tie together one bay leaf, a good sprig of thyme and two stalks of parsley, using a long thin string or thick thread.

DRYING HERBS

Dry herbs in the dark and in a warm atmosphere such as a low oven or airing cupboard at approximately 38°C/100°F/Gas ¼. The air must circulate freely around the drying herbs.

FREEZING HERBS

The general rule for freezing is that only the leafy herbs such as parsley, chervil, coriander and sage retain their colour and flavour really well.

Small packets of frozen herbs can easily be crumbled into sauces during cooking. The spiky leaves of thyme and rosemary are probably better dried.

Some fresh herbs can be frozen in ice-cube trays. Mint cubes, for example, are delicious in summer drinks.

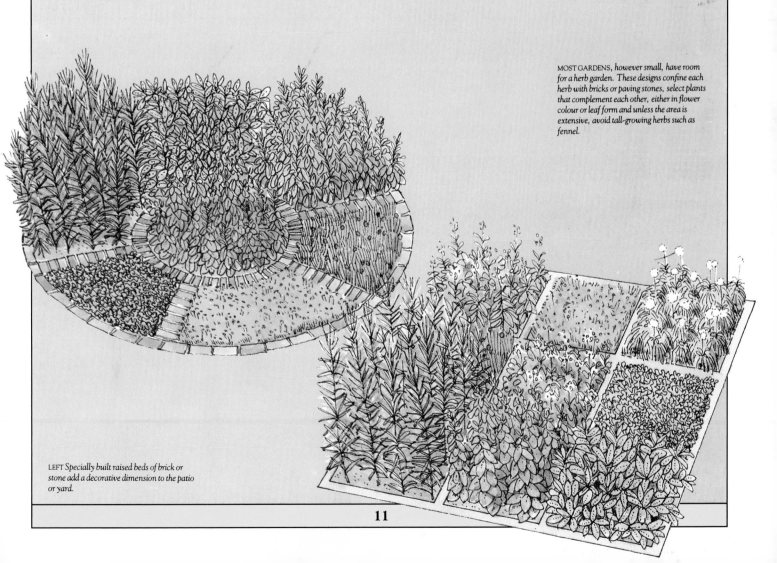

MOST GARDENS, *however small, have room for a herb garden. These designs confine each herb with bricks or paving stones, select plants that complement each other, either in flower colour or leaf form and unless the area is extensive, avoid tall-growing herbs such as fennel.*

LEFT *Specially built raised beds of brick or stone add a decorative dimension to the patio or yard.*

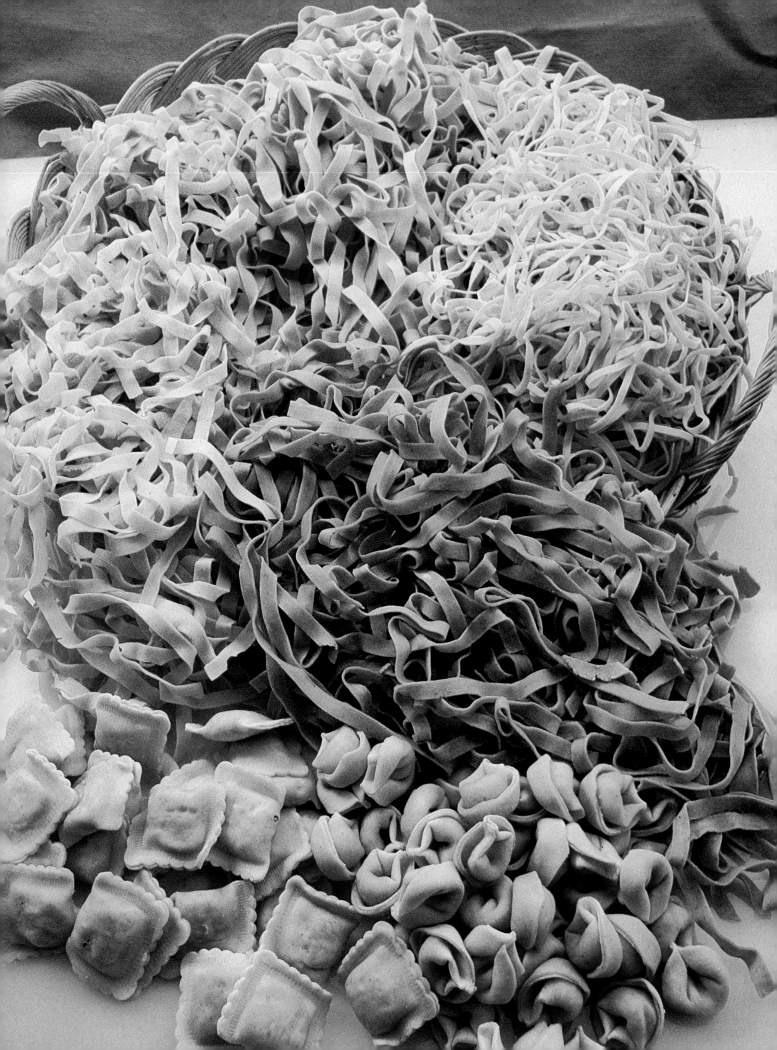

PASTA

The popularity of fresh pasta is growing steadily with the opening of fresh pasta shops everywhere. Supermarkets now stock a wide range of pre-packed fresh pasta.

Making pasta is simple once the technique is familiar and many people are now making it at home. With or without the help of some relatively inexpensive equipment, which is shown on the following pages, pasta making is fun. There is no doubt that making your own stuffed pasta ensures a wider variety and better quality in the fillings. Anyone who can make pastry can make pasta with a little practice.

In Italy most housewives use both fresh and dried pasta and this seems an excellent idea as one always has cupboard ingredients for a quick pasta meal.

PASTA DOUGH
Ingredients
4½ cups/450 g/1 lb plain flour
½ tsp salt
2 eggs
1 tbsp olive oil
5-7 tbsp warm water
Makes 450 g/1 lb

1 Sieve the flour on to a clean table or pastry board.

2 Make a well in the centre of the flour and fill it with the eggs, oil and a little of the water. Mix the well contents with a spatula.

3 Mix the dough gradually, by hand, by pulling the flour in to the egg mixture. Form a second well in the centre and add the water as needed to make a firm smooth paste.

4 Knead well for several minutes and then rest the dough, covered with a cloth before rolling.

This mixture can be used to hand-roll and make lasagne, cannelloi, ravioli, capelleti etc. It is also suitable for use with a hand-cranked rolling and cutting machine (see page 19).

To make spinach pasta, substitute 2 tbsp of water with 2 tbsp of spinach purée.

To make tomato pasta substitute 1 tbsp of tomato purée, or more if a darker colour is desired.

1 Sieve the flour on to a clean surface, make a well in the centre of the flour large enough to hold the eggs. Add the eggs and a little oil.

2 Sprinkle flour over the eggs and stir with a spatula. Add the water gradually, stirring the mixture around with some added flour. Pull a little flour from the sides to cover the egg mixture.

3 Start to mix the dough by pulling the flour on to the egg mixture gradually until it is all mixed in. If the mixture is too stiff, add a few drops of water to take up all the flour. Take care not to make the mixture too wet.

4 Knead the dough for several minutes with the heel of the hand until it can be formed into a smooth ball. Divide the ball in two and rest for a few minutes in the refrigerator. Now clean the board and make sure it is quite dry for rolling out the dough.

5 Sprinkle with flour. Take one piece of dough and roll it out into a rectangular or oval shape. Keep turning it and flour it regularly underneath; try to keep it the same width as the rolling pin. Roll the dough as thin as you can. For tagliatelli you should be able to see the table through it. Leave to rest for about 40 minutes before cutting.

MAKING PASTA DOUGH BY HAND

TO CUT TAGLIATELLI

Cut strips with a ruler about ½ cm (¼ in) wide. This takes rather a long time but is very simple.

Alternatively roll the sheet of dough up and with a sharp knife cut ½-cm (¼-in) slices. Unroll the slices and leave on a tray until the pasta is ready to be cooked (see page 22).

The pasta will be cooked in about 2 minutes, but always test it before draining.

CUTTING LASAGNE

Roll the dough thinly as described above. Cut 5-cm (2-in) strips with a ruler and a sharp knife. The size can be altered to suit the dish in which the lasagne is to be cooked.

To cook, drop the strips into a large saucepan of boiling water with salt and oil. Boil for 2 minutes, drain and lay out on a tray ready to make up the dishes with sauces (see page 26).

MAKING PASTA BOWS

Cut the thin pasta into 2½-cm (1-in) squares (or a little smaller if you prefer small bows) using a pastry wheel. With two fingers squeeze the centre of the square to make the bow shape.

Allow to dry for a few minutes before cooking.

Cook in boiling salted water with a few drops of oil added to prevent sticking. Test after 2 minutes.

TO MAKE CAPPELLETTI

These little pasta hats are stuffed with a filling which can be either cheese, meat or chicken based.

1 Cut the thinly rolled pasta into 4-cm (1½-in) squares. If you are cooking with machine-made pasta use the lasagne cutter to extrude strips which can be cut into squares. Place the filling in the centre of the squares and brush the edges of each with water.

2 Fold over in a triangle. Twist round into the little hat shape.

TO MAKE TORTELLINI

Cut out rounds with a pastry cutter 4 cm (1½ in) in diameter. Place the stuffing in the middle, brush the edge with water, fold in half to make a crescent shape. Shape around a finger.

For stuffings see page 18.

Both cappelletti and tortellini can be kept for a day or two before being cooked. If storing in the fridge, cover with a plastic wrap.

Cook in boiling salted water, with a few drops of oil added, for about 7 minutes. Start testing after 5 minutes as the cooking time will depend on the size and the thickness of the pasta.

STUFFINGS

VEAL AND CHICKEN STUFFING

VEAL AND CHICKEN STUFFING
1 small onion, peeled
1 clove garlic, crushed
2 tbsp oil
⅓ cup/50 g/2 oz cooked chicken
½ cup/100 g/4 oz minced (ground) veal
1 tbsp fresh breadcrumbs
1 tbsp parmesan cheese
salt and freshly ground pepper
½ tsp brandy (optional)
1 tsp chopped parsley
a few spikes of fresh rosemary
a few leaves fresh or 1 tsp dried thyme
½ egg, beaten
For 450 g/1 lb pasta dough

1 Dice the onion finely, crush the garlic.

2 Heat the oil and cook the onion and garlic for 4 minutes over a low heat until transparent. Remove with a slotted spoon into a bowl.

3 Place the minced veal in the oil and fry over a medium heat for 5 minutes, separating with a fork as it cooks; add the chicken for the last 2 minutes. Spoon into the bowl.

4 Add all the remaining ingredients and mix well with the egg. Allow to cool and use as required for stuffing pasta.

RICOTTA AND PARMESAN STUFFING

RICOTTA AND PARMESAN STUFFING
1⅓ cups/225 g/8 oz ricotta cheese
⅓ cup/50 g/2 oz parmesan cheese
2 tbsp chopped parsley
1 tbsp fresh breadcrumbs
¼ tsp nutmeg
½ tsp marjoram
salt and freshly ground pepper
1 egg, beaten
For 450 g/1 lb pasta dough

1 Mix all the ingredients in a bowl and add the egg slowly so that the mixture does not become too wet.

2 Use as required to stuff pasta shapes.

RICOTTA AND SPINACH STUFFING

Use 1 cup/75 g/7 oz ricotta cheese. Drain ⅓-½ cup/100 g/4 oz fresh, frozen or canned spinach. Chop and mix with other ingredients.

1 Mark the rolled dough (which has not been allowed to rest after rolling) with a pastry wheel into 2½-cm/1-in squares. Place the stuffing in the squares and top with the other strip of pasta. Cut around the squares with the wheel and place on a flat tray.

2 To make the ravioli in a shaped tray, roll the pasta in to strips a little larger than the tray, line the tray with pasta and place the filling in each of the square sections. Cover the whole with another strip and roll over the top with a rolling pin. The ravioli shapes will seal and the tray can be turned over to release the ravioli.

The ravioli can be kept covered in a plastic wrap until cooked. Cook in boiling salted water for about 6 minutes, testing after 4 minutes.

ROLLING THE DOUGH WITH A MACHINE

1 Split the dough into 3 portions, feeding each one through the machine at a time. Fold into 3 as it comes out of the machine. After feeding the pasta through the rollers at their widest setting, flour it lightly if it becomes sticky. Set the rollers closer together and feed through again. You will have a long strip by now, which may become awkward to handle, so cut in half at this stage.

2 When the dough reaches the required thinness, cut it into 25-cm (10-in) strips and feed them through the shredding rollers to make fettucini.

3 Take the strips out when cut and lay them on a floured tray or hang them over a rolling pin or piece of wood to dry for about 30 minutes; drying them out slightly will prevent the pasta sticking together.

It is possible to cut lasagne and tagliatelli to different widths on this machine and there is also an attachment for making spaghetti and ravioli.

1 If you find pasta-making too energetic, a variety of electric machines are available to do the job for you from start to finish. It is essential to use the recipes given with each machine as the consistency of the dough varies for each one.

2 Ingredients for egg, spinach and tomato pasta. The white plastic mixing disc is held in the hand.

3 The flour is fed into the machine.

4 The finished consistency of the dough is completely different from that of hand-made pasta. It must be lumpy without being sticky to ensure the efficient running of the machine.

5 The machine is now fitted with the appropriate disc (in this case the macaroni disc). The pasta can be cut off at the desired length with a sharp knife.

6 Tomato macaroni and egg macaroni are being extruded.

MAKING PASTA WITH ATTACHMENT FOR ELECTRIC MIXER

1 The pasta dough must be made to the recipe supplied with the appliance. Assemble all the ingredients in the right quantities — a special measuring jug for the eggs and water is supplied with the attachment.

2 Mix the ingredients in the bowl of the machine using the K-beater. Add the egg gradually with the machine switched on. The pasta will mix to a lumpy consistency as shown in the picture.

3 The picture shows the consistency required before extrusion but after the kneading process has been completed. Remove the bowl and fit the pasta attachment at the front of the machine.

4 The dough is pushed down the funnel with the tool provided and converted into spaghetti by the spaghetti disc. Lay the pasta on floured trays or hang over a chair back or rolling pin to dry off for 30 minutes.

Pasta, like any other food, can be ruined during the cooking period. It is simple to cook but care must be taken to arrive at a pasta which is cooked to perfection. Cooking instructions are given on most packets of commercially produced pasta and on the chilled fresh variety on sale at many supermarkets. These instructions are, however, only a rough guide. The pasta cook must test as the cooking progresses to achieve the perfectly cooked pasta, known in Italy as *al dente*. This means literally 'to the tooth'; pasta should be cooked until still slightly chewy and resilient. It should be neither too hard nor too soft and should not taste of flour.

Italian enthusiasts may prefer pasta less cooked than others, but taste varies so much from individual to individual that it is essential to try the pasta as it is cooking by biting through a test piece. This way you can tell when the pasta is done to your taste. It may be necessary to try it three times to make sure it is cooked just right.

You will need a large saucepan to cook 500 g/1 lb pasta. People who cook pasta frequently usually have a very large saucepan. The pasta tends to stick together if there is too little water in the saucepan.

The guide for cooking pasta can be calculated on a basis of 5 cups/1.2 l/2 pts water to 1 cup/125 g/4 oz pasta. This means that you will need approximately 20 cups/4.8 l/8 pts water for 450 g/1 lb. Many experts insist on even more water than this but one has to be practical in today's modern kitchens. But a 30-cup/7.2-l/12-pt pan is beyond the storage capacity of most kitchens. You may find it better to cook 2 cups/225 g/8 oz pasta at a time in an average 10-cup/2.4-l/1/4-pt saucepan.

1 Bring the water to the boil, adding 1½ tsp salt for each 5 cups/1.2 l/2 pts water once it has boiled.

2 Add 1 tsp oil to each 5 cups/1.2 l/2 pts water to prevent pasta sticking together.

3 Turn heat on to full to keep the water boiling and add pasta gradually, making sure it is all under the water. Long dried pasta should be introduced gradually; as one part softens, push down the next to avoid breaking.

4 Stir around gently with a wooden fork to avoid breaking and to make sure the pasta does not stick together. Fresh pasta must be separated gently before cooking if it has been sitting in a bag or box.

5 Take cooking time given on pack as guide and taste at least 3 minutes before the end of this given time for dried pasta. Continue tasting until pasta is just right. If small shapes such as macaroni and small shells take 7-8 minutes, start testing after 5 minutes.

6 Fresh pasta will take a much shorter time than dried and must be tested after the first 5 minutes for stuffed pasta and after about 1½ minutes for fettuccini and tagliatelli.

7 Drain the pasta and toss in a little melted butter. Do not rinse pasta under cold water unless you want to cool it quickly for a salad.

8 A shake of freshly milled pepper and a grating of nutmeg will enhance the flavour of the pasta.

9 Keep pasta warm by using heated bowls or plates and serve piping hot. Cold pasta can be delicious but the lukewarm pasta with lukewarm sauce beloved of so many restaurants is not.

QUANTITIES

Allow ½ cup/50 g/2 oz (uncooked) per person for a starter (appetizer).

Most small to average appetites are satisfied with ¾ cup/75 g/3 oz pasta per person. Average to hearty appetites may need ¾-1 cup/85-100 g/3½-4 oz per person. You will need approximately 2½ cups/600 ml/1 pt sauce for 450/1 lb pasta.

If you are catering for a party, remember that quantities can be reduced; 20 people will not need as much as you may think. 4 people will need 450 g/1 lb spaghetti, 2½ cups/600 ml/1 pt sauce and ⅓ cup/50 g/2 oz cheese.

20 people will need approximately 1.7 kg/3¾ lb pasta, 10 cups/2.4 l/4 pts sauce and 1⅓ cups/225 g/8 oz grated parmesan cheese. These quantities can be reduced further if there is a choice of other dishes.

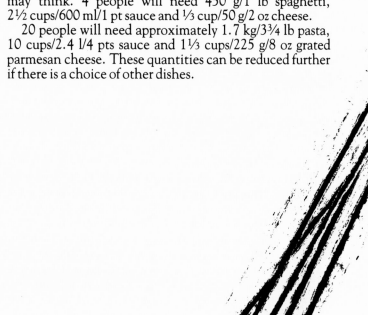

SPECIAL DISHES

MAKING LASAGNE

1 Place 4 tbsp bolognese sauce on the bottom of the dish and top it with 3 tbsp bechamel sauce and three strips of cooked lasagne. If using dried, the non-cook variety should be placed directly on the sauces. Season the pasta with salt and pepper.

2 Start the layers of sauce again as shown in the picture. Use another 3 tbsp bolognese sauce and 3 tbsp bechamel.

3 Top with another 3 strips of lasagne, a further 3 tbsp bolognese sauce and 3 tbsp bechamel. Add remaining strips of lasagne, season and spread the meat sauce on top of the final topping of white sauce.

4 Spread the bechamel over the surface and sprinkle it with grated parmesan cheese or parmesan cheese mixed with dried breadcrumbs to give a crunchy topping when cooked.

LASAGNE AL FORNO

Ingredients

9 sheets cooked fresh lasagne

2 cups/450 ml/¾ pt bolognese sauce (page 45)

2½ cups/600/1 pt bechamel sauce (page 38)

1 tbsp dried breadcrumbs

1 tbsp parmesan cheese

salt and pepper

Oven temperature 180°C/350°F/Gas 4.

To prepare

1 Follow the steps given with the pictures until the dish is filled. The dish used in these pictures is 25 cm (10 in) long × 20 cm (8 in) wide and will provide 4 main course portions or 6 starters.

2 Bake the lasagne for 25 minutes until golden brown. If you prefer a really brown cheesy top, the dish can be put under the grill (broiler) for 3 minutes.

Serves 4

VEGETABLE LASAGNE

Ingredients

4 tbsp oil

1 aubergine (eggplant), sliced

1 red pepper, seeded

1 courgette (zucchini), sliced

salt and freshly ground pepper

2 cups/100 g/4 oz mushrooms sliced

2 cups/¾ pt pomodoro sauce (page 43)

2½ cups/600 ml/1 pt bechamel sauce (page 38)

9 sheets cooked lasagne (page 16)

Oven temperature 180°C/350°F/Gas 4.

To prepare

1 Heat the oil and fry the vegetables over a low heat filling the pan and turning in the oil for about 3 minutes each batch. You will need to allow 15 minutes for preparing and frying the vegetables.

2 Start with the pomodori sauce and one third of the vegetables. Top with bechamel sauce and lasagne. Season and start layering as in lasagne al forno ending with bechamel and cheese.

3 When all the ingredients are used, bake until golden brown in the oven for 25 minutes.

Serves 4

MAKING CANNELLONI

1 Put the spinach and ricotta cheese mixture into a piping bag with a 1¼-cm (½-in) plain nozzle. If you do not want to use a piping bag, spoon the pasta with a teaspoon. Lay the uncooked pasta strips (7½ cm/2½ in wide) on a board. Pipe the mixture along the width of the pasta, roll into a round tube, cut with a sharp knife.

2 Place the pomodoro sauce in the bottom of the dish, arrange the tubes on top and season the cannelloni.

3 When all the pasta tubes are arranged in the pomodoro sauce, pour the bechamel on top covering the pasta completely.

4 Sprinkle with parmesan cheese and bake in the oven for 30 minutes.

SPINACH AND RICOTTA CANNELLONI

Ingredients
½-¾ cup/175 g/6 oz chopped spinach, cooked
⅔ cup/100 g/4 oz ricotta cheese
salt and freshly ground pepper
1 tbsp fresh breadcrumbs
1 tsp parmesan cheese
¼ tsp marjoram
¼ tsp nutmeg
6 strips fresh pasta
⅓ cup/50 g/2 oz parmesan cheese
Oven temperature 180°C/350°F/Gas 4.

To prepare

1 Mix the cooked spinach, which can be fresh, frozen or canned, with the ricotta cheese in a bowl. Season and add the breadcrumbs, marjoram and nutmeg and 1 tsp parmesan cheese. Cream to a smooth mixture.

2 Use in the piping bag as directed in the step-by-step pictures (opposite).

3 Cook for 25 minutes.

Serves 4

POTATO GNOCCHI

Ingredients
3 cups/450 g/1 lb cooked potatoes, sliced
2¼ cups/225 g/8 oz plain flour
salt and pepper
2 tbsp/25 g/1 oz melted butter

To prepare

1 Put the cooked boiled potatoes through a large sieve or mouli. Add the sieved plain flour with some seasoning and the melted butter. Mix together.

2 Turn onto a floured board and knead lightly until you have an elastic dough. Divide into 2½-cm (1-in) pieces and make into little rolls. Shape by pulling the end pieces towards you.

3 Cook in boiling salted water for about 10 minutes. Serve with a piquant well flavoured sauce and cheese. Dot the gnocchi alternately with butter and sprinkled cheese and cook in the oven until golden brown.

Serves 4-6

SHAPING *the gnocchi.*

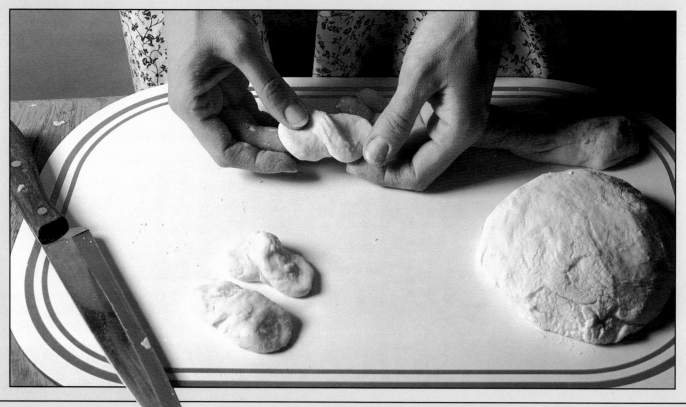

LEFT Gnocchi with tomato sauce.   *RIGHT Gnocchi with mozzarella cheese.*

Ingredients

1 cup/450 g/1 lb cooked spinach
1⅓ cups/225 g/8 oz ricotta cheese
⅓ cup/50 g/2 oz parmesan cheese
salt and freshly ground pepper
1 tbsp/15 g/½ oz butter
4 tbsp plain flour
¼ tsp ground nutmeg

To prepare

1 Drain the cooked spinach well. Either chop finely or add gradually to a blender or food processor. The mixture must be creamed together with the cheese — this will take only a few seconds in the machine.

2 Mix the eggs in a bowl and season well and add the sieved flour and nutmeg. Add the spinach mixture and mix well. The food processor will mix the dough.

3 Leave in the refrigerator for at least half an hour, preferably longer, to chill.

4 Flour a pastry-board or work-top and knead the mixture for a few minutes with floured hands. Take small pieces and roll into 5-cm (2-in) lengths.

5 Drop the gnocchi into a saucepan of boiling salted water and cook for about 10 minutes. Drain well and serve with a little melted butter and parmesan cheese.

Serves 4

FETTUCINI ROMA

Ingredients

450 g/1 lb fettucini

4 tbsp/50 g/2 oz butter

½ tsp ground nutmeg

⅝ cup/150 ml/¼ pt cream

salt and freshly ground pepper

⅔ cup/100 g/4 oz parmesan cheese

To prepare

1 Bring a well filled saucepan of salted water to the boil, add a few drops of oil and salt. Feed in the fettucini and cook until *al dente* — fresh pasta will only take about 2 minutes. Drain in a colander.

2 Melt the butter in the saucepan, add ground nutmeg. Pour in half the cream and stir until shiny and bubbles start to appear.

3 Add the fettucini and stir around in the pan. Pour in the remaining cream and cheese alternately, forking the pasta as it is mixed. Serve immediately.

Note

This is a real pasta-lovers' dish. To obtain best results use freshly grated parmesan cheese rather than the commercially grated variety.

Serves 4

Pasta trio

Ingredients

1⅓ cups/225 g/ 8 oz stuffed ravioli or tortellini

1¼ cups/300 ml/½ pt bechamel sauce

1 cup/225 g/8 oz tagliatelli

1 cup/225 ml/8 oz pomodoro sauce (page 43)

1 cup/225 g/8 oz wholewheat twistetti

1¼ cups/300 ml/½ pt bolognese sauce (page 45)

To garnish

⅔ cup/100 g/4 oz parmesan cheese

To prepare

1 Cook the pasta, starting with that which has the longest cooking time, drain the water into a bowl and return the pasta to the saucepan and keep it warm.

2 Keep the three sauces warm.

3 Serve on individual dishes on a large plate accompanied by a bowl of parmesan cheese and green salad.

For this dish you can serve any of your favourite pastas and sauces

Serves 4

Variations

Fettucini and pesto

Spaghetti Bolognese

Ravioli and Tomato Sauce

Capelletti and Broth

Tagliatelli Bolognese

Spaghetti alla Carbonara

Ravioli with Cream and Cheese

Cannelloni with Spinach and Ricotta Sauce

Wholewheat Spaghetti with Bolognese Sauce or
Tomato Sauce for a vegetarian meal

SPAGHETTI ALLE VONGOLE

Ingredients

1 onion, peeled

2 cloves garlic, crushed

4 tbsp olive oil

6 beef tomatoes, peeled and diced or
1½ cups/425 g/15 oz canned tomatoes

4 tbsp white wine

salt and freshy ground pepper

1 small can clams

2 tbsp freshly chopped parsley

¾ lb/350 g/12 oz spaghetti

1 tbsp/15 g/½ oz butter

pinch of nutmeg

To prepare

1 Dice the onion finely, peel and crush the garlic. Heat the oil in saucepan or large frying pan and cook over a low heat until the onion is transparent.

2 Add the tomatoes, white wine and seasoning. Simmer for 10 minutes. Add the drained clams and heat gently for a further 6 minutes.

3 Meanwhile cook the spaghetti in plenty of boiling salted water for about 12 minutes. Drain and toss in a little melted butter, add a shake of pepper and nutmeg.

4 Add the parsley to the sauce and stir well. Combine with the clam sauce and serve at once on heated plates.

If you are using fresh clams scrub the shells and wash well in several batches of cold water to remove sand and grit. Place them in a frying pan with 2 tbsp of white wine and cook over a high heat until the shells open. Strain and use the juice in the sauce. Remove the fish from the shells and heat through in the sauce as in **2** above.

Serves 4

Variation

Add 3 tbsp single cream (cereal cream) to the sauce before serving.

SAUCES

Most people enjoy pasta with sauce and the more unusual sauces as well as the old favourites, served with different pastas, can add endless variety to everyday meals.
The Italians are known for their use of fresh young vegetables and it is the fresh ingredients which makes even the most simple sauce, served with well cooked pasta, a feast. Everyone can add creativity to pasta meals by experimenting with fresh vegetables. It is not essential to serve pasta only with tomato-based sauces.
When preparing sauces with vegetables, it is as well to remember to serve pasta of a similar size to that of the sauce ingredients. It is difficult to pick up small pasta with chunky vegetables.
Use fresh tomatoes when possible but when they are expensive and lacking in flavour there is little point; however a few fresh tomatoes added to the canned variety does give a sauce a fresh flavour.

BECHAMEL SAUCE

Ingredients

2½ cups/600 ml/1 pt milk
1 small onion, peeled
1 small carrot, peeled and sliced
1 bay leaf
6 slightly crushed peppercorns
1 blade of mace
1 stalk parsley
3 tbsp/40 g/1½ oz butter
6 tbsp/40 g/1½ oz flour
salt and white pepper

To prepare

1 Pour milk into a saucepan. Add the onion cut into quarters with 2 slices of carrot, bay leaf, peppercorns, mace and parsley stalk.

2 Cover and allow to heat on a low heat without boiling for about 10 minutes. Remove from the heat and allow to infuse for a further 10 minutes, covered.

3 Make a roux (a blend of butter and flour) by melting the butter in a saucepan. Do not allow the butter to brown. Add the flour and stir well over a medium heat.

4 Gradually add the strained milk and stir briskly or whisk until a smooth creamy sauce is made, season to taste.

Makes 2½ cups/600 ml/1 pt sauce

Variation
MORNAY SAUCE

2 egg yolks
2 tbsp cream
2½ cups/600 ml/1 pt bechamel sauce
⅓ cup/50 g/2 oz grated parmesan cheese

To prepare

1 Mix the egg yolks with the cream and add a little warm bechamel return to the warm bechamel sauce stir well.

2 Lastly fold in the grated cheese.

SAUCES

TUNA AND MUSHROOM SAUCE

Ingredients

2 tbsp/25 g/1 oz butter

1 tbsp oil

1¾ cups/100 g/4 oz mushrooms, washed

generous 1 cup/200 g/7 oz canned tuna fish

2 tsp tomato purée

2 tbsp white wine

2½ cups/600 ml/1 pt bechamel sauce

salt and freshly ground pepper

To prepare

1 Heat the butter and oil and cook the mushrooms for 3 minutes, turning from time to time.

2 Flake the tuna fish.

3 Add the tomato purée, white wine to the bechamel sauce, mix well.

4 Over a low heat re-heat the sauce and gradually stir in the tuna fish and the drained mushrooms. Cook gently for a few minutes until well mixed and hot. Taste and adjust seasoning.

Mix the sauce with 450 g/1 lb cooked pasta.

Makes 1⅞ cups/750 ml/1¼ pt sauce

Tuna and mushroom sauce

BLUE CHEESE SAUCE

Ingredients

2½ cups/600 ml/1 pt bechamel sauce (page 38)

⅔ cup/100 g/4 oz Roquefort or other blue cheese

salt and freshly ground pepper

½ tsp French mustard

pinch of cayenne pepper

To prepare

1 Make up the bechamel sauce.

2 Crumble the cheese and add to the sauce. Stir over a low heat.

3 Taste for seasoning. Add salt and pepper to taste and then the mustard. Lastly stir in the pinch of cayenne.

This sauce will accompany approximately 3-4 cups/ 450-750 g/1-1½ lb cooked pasta.

Makes 1⅞ cups/750 ml/1¼ pt sauce

Spinach and ricotta sauce

SPINACH AND RICOTTA SAUCE

Ingredients

1¼ cups/300 ml/½ pt bechamel sauce (page 38)

½ cup/225 g/8 oz (after cooking), fresh or frozen spinach

⅔ cup/100 g/4 oz ricotta cheese

½ tsp nutmeg

salt and freshly ground pepper

To prepare

1 Make up the bechamel sauce.

2 Cook the spinach for a few minutes and then drain well. Squeeze against the collander to remove the liquid.
   You will need to cook approx 750 g/1½ lb fresh spinach to be left with the amount required by the recipe. Chop or liquidize.

3 Mix the ricotta with the spinach and season well, add nutmeg.

4 Gradually stir into the bechamel sauce and re-heat carefully over a low heat.

Serve with approximately 3-4 cups/500-750 g/1-1½ lb cooked pasta.
   This sauce is also delicious used in a vegetable or chicken lasagne.

Makes approximately 2½ cups/600 ml/1 pt sauce

SAUCES

TOMATO SAUCE

Ingredients
2 tbsp oil
1 large onion, peeled and diced
1-2 cloves garlic, peeled and crushed
2 stalks celery, washed
1 carrot, scraped and grated
1½ cups/ 425 g/15 oz canned tomatoes
1½ cups/450 g/1 lb tomatoes, skinned and chopped
1 bouquet garni
1 bay leaf
1 tbsp fresh or ½ tsp dried basil, chopped
1 stalk parsley
½ tsp sugar
1¼ cups/300 ml/½ pt chicken or beef stock
2 tbsp red wine
salt and freshly ground pepper

To prepare

1 Heat the oil in a saucepan and cook the onions over a low heat for 5 minutes until transparent. Add crushed garlic to onions.

2 Remove the strings from the celery stalks with a sharp knife and chop into small pieces, add to the onion.

3 Add all other ingredients, bring to the boil, lower the heat and simmer for 40 minutes.

4 Remove bouquet garni, bay leaf and parsley stalk and serve with pasta.

For a smooth sauce pass through a sieve or blender.

Makes approximately 2½ cups/600 ml/1 pt

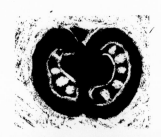   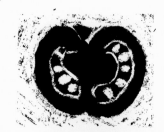

TOMATO (POMODORO) SAUCE

Ingredients

1 onion, peeled and finely chopped
2 cloves garlic, crushed
1 carrot, scraped and grated
2 tbsp freshly chopped parsley
1 tbsp freshly chopped basil
1 bay leaf
4½ cups/1½ kg/3 lb large tomatoes, skinned and chopped
4 tbsp dry white wine

To prepare

1 Place all the ingredients in a thick saucepan and simmer for 20 minutes until the tomatoes are puréed.

2 Sieve the sauce or pass through an electric blender or food processor. Taste for seasoning and adjust.

This fresh tomato sauce is really best made with large ripe beef tomatoes and fresh basil. The taste with fresh pasta is delicious.

Serves 4

TOMATO (MARINARA) SAUCE

Ingredients

4 tbsp olive oil
2 cloves garlic, crushed
4½ cups/1½ kg/3 lb ripe beef tomatoes, peeled and chopped
salt and freshly ground pepper
6 basil leaves

To prepare

1 Heat the oil in a saucepan, add the garlic and stir for 1 minute. Add the tomatoes roughly chopped and seasoning and allow to simmer for 6 minutes.

2 Chop the basil leaves and add to the tomatoes, stir the sauce for a further minute. Serve on freshly cooked pasta. This sauce is a simple accompaniment to pasta which is very good to eat and easy to prepare but the secret is that the tomatoes should be simply heated through, not cooked to a pulp.

Serves 4

PEPPER SAUCE

Ingredients
1 red pepper, seeded
1 green pepper, seeded
1 tbsp chopped parsley
1¼ cups/300 ml/½ pt tomato sauce, liquidized

To prepare

1 Dice the seeded peppers quite fine. Add to the liquidized tomato sauce with 4 tbsp stock or water and simmer for 10 minutes.

2 Add chopped parsley and use alone with pasta or with meat or fish accompanying pasta.

Makes approximately 2½ cups/600 ml/1 pt

Ingredients
1 large onion, peeled and diced
1 carrot, scraped and grated
1 stalk celery, washed and chopped
2 cloves garlic, crushed
2 slices bacon
1 tbsp oil
½ cup/100 g/4 oz lean minced (ground) beef
½ cup/100 g/4 oz lean minced (ground) veal
1¼ cups/300 ml/½ pt beef stock or water
1½ cups/425 g/15 oz canned tomatoes
4 tomatoes, skinned and chopped
1 bay leaf
1 tsp origanum
½ tsp basil
1 bouquet garni
salt and freshly ground pepper
1 tbsp tomato purée
⅝ cup/150 ml/¼ pt red wine

To prepare

1 Prepare the vegetables making sure that they are diced very fine. Remove strings from the celery with a sharp knife before chopping.

2 Cut the bacon into small pieces having first removed the rind.

3 Heat the oil in the pan and brown all the meat over a medium heat. Remove with a slotted spoon leaving any fat behind.

4 Cook the vegetables in the meat fat adding a little extra oil if necessary, over a low heat for 5 minutes.

5 Put the meat and vegetables into a saucepan with the tomatoes, herbs and seasoning. Lastly add the tomato purée and stir in the wine.

6 Bring to the boil and simmer gently for 45 minutes. Remove bouquet garni and bay leaf before serving.

Serve with spaghetti and other pastas with parmesan cheese served separately.

Bolognese sauce

Serves 4

RAGU SAUCE

Ingredients
1 onion, peeled
2 cloves garlic, crushed
1 carrot, scraped and grated
1 stalk celery
6 tomatoes, peeled and chopped or 1½ cups/425 g/15 oz canned tomatoes
4 tbsp oil
1 cup/225 g/8 oz lean minced (ground) beef
½ cup/100 g/4 oz chicken livers
1 bouquet garni
1 bay leaf
1¼ cups/300 ml/½ pt stock and red wine
1 tsp origanum
1 stalk parsley

To prepare

1 Prepare the vegetables. Cut the onion finely, coarsely grate the carrot. Wash the celery and remove strings with a sharp knife before chopping into very small pieces. Prepare tomatoes.

2 Heat half the oil in a saucepan and cook the onion and garlic for 3 minutes over a low heat. Add carrot and celery, stir into the oil and allow to cook for a further 3 minutes.

3 Heat the remaining oil in a frying pan and brown the beef well over a high heat. Turn the heat down to medium and add chopped chicken livers. Mix with the beef and cook until brown.

4 Add the meat to the vegetables with the herbs and wine, season well, add the stock and simmer for 45 minutes. Taste for seasoning before serving with freshly cooked pasta.

Serves 4

SAUCES

PUTANESCA SAUCE

Ingredients
1 onion, peeled and diced
2 tbsp oil
1 carrot, scraped and chopped
1½ cups/425 g/15 oz canned tomatoes
2 tomatoes, skinned and chopped
4 tbsp white wine
1 bay leaf
3-4 basil leaves or 1 tsp dried basil
salt and freshly ground pepper
1 tbsp capers, chopped
1 small can anchovies
½ cup/50 g/2 oz stoned black olives
3 drops Tabasco sauce
1 tbsp freshly chopped parsley

To prepare

1 Put the onion into the oil in a frying saucepan over a low heat.

2 Allow to cook gently for 4 minutes, add the crushed garlic and carrots. Turn in the oil for another minute.

3 Add the tomatoes, the white wine, bay leaf, basil, some seasoning and 4 anchovy fillets

4 Bring to the boil and simmer for 30 minutes. Sieve or liquidize into a measuring jug.

5 Return to the saucepan and add chopped capers, the remainder of the anchovies chopped into small pieces, chopped olives and the spicy Tabasco sauce. Re-heat gently.

Serve with 450 g/1 lb cooked pasta with parmesan cheese served separately.

Makes 2½ cups/600 ml/1 pt sauce

GENOESE PESTO SAUCE

Ingredients

2 tbsp/25 g/1 oz fresh basil leaves

2 cloves garlic

pinch of salt

½ cup/50 g/2 oz pine kernels

⅓ cup/50 g/2 oz parmesan cheese

½ cup/100 ml/4 fl oz olive oil

To prepare

1 Blend the basil leaves in a liquidizer. Add the crushed cloves of garlic and olive oil. Process for a few seconds.

2 Gradually add the pine kernels, parmesan cheese, season remembering that Parmesan has a salty taste. The consistency should be thick and creamy.

Note

This sauce was originally made by grinding the basil with the garlic salt and pine nuts in a pestle and mortar into a purée. Add the cheese and the oil gradually.

Even in summer it is not always easy to obtain a great deal of basil and although the flavour is different, fresh parsley and basil together can be substituted.

This quantity of pesto will be sufficient for 450 g/1 lb cooked drained pasta. Melt 2 tbsp/25 g/1 oz butter in the saucepan and re-heat the cooked pasta. Remove from the heat and mix 2 tbsp pesto with the pasta. Serve on individual plates with a spoonful of pesto on each helping. Parmesan can be added last.

The pesto is never heated. It can be served on pasta at the table but make sure the pasta is hot when served.

Makes 1¼ cups/300 ml/½ pt sauce

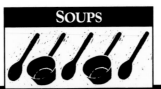

SOUPS

WINTER PESTO SAUCE

Ingredients
½ cup/50 g/2 oz fresh parsley
2 cloves garlic
½ cup/50 g/2 oz pine kernels
⅓ cup/50 g/2 oz parmesan cheese
salt and freshly ground pepper
2 tsp dried basil
⅝ cup/150 ml/¼ pt olive oil

To prepare

1 Chop the parsley finely in the blender or with a sharp knife if making by hand.

2 Add the garlic crushed to the blender and process for a few seconds. Gradually add the other ingredients through the top of the machine while it is running. When the mixture is puréed add a little olive oil at a time.

3 Add the dried basil when half the oil has been added. Continue adding oil until a thick creamy mixture is made.

To make by hand see Genoese Pesto Sauce .

Makes approximately 1¼ cups/300 ml/½ pt

MAYONNAISE

Ingredients
2 egg yolks
1¼ cups/300 ml/½ pt olive oil
½ tsp salt
pinch of white pepper
pinch of dried mustard
1 tbsp wine vinegar or lemon juice

To prepare

1 Make sure the eggs are used at room temperature and not taken directly from the refrigerator. Warm a clean dry bowl slightly for the egg yolks, mix for a few seconds.

2 Gradually add the oil, drop by drop to begin with. Mix briskly with a wooden spoon or a small wire whisk. The mixture will become a thick creamy emulsion as the drops of oil are added.

3 When the mixture has thickened add the seasoning with a few drops of vinegar or lemon juice. Beat well. The mayonnaise can be made thicker or thinner according to the amount of vinegar or lemon juice used. Taste for seasoning before using.

Note

To mix with pasta, a little more lemon juice may be used, as a thinner sauce is better for coating the cooked pasta.

Makes 1¼ cups/300 ml/½ pt

SOUPS

Soups with pasta as an ingredient served with grated cheese make hearty meals by themselves and are ideal for lunches and snacks. There is nothing more cheering on a cold day than a bowl of fresh vegetable soup. There are many small pasta shapes available which are suitable for soup but if you do not have any in stock, spaghetti can always be broken into small lengths.

Ingredients

2 onions, peeled and sliced
2 carrots, scraped and sliced
3 stalks celery
2 bay leaves
2 stalks parsley
1 bouquet garni
6 peppercorns, slightly crushed
1½-kg/3-lb boiling fowl
15-20 cups/3.5-5 l/6-8 pt water

To prepare

1 Place all ingredients in a large saucepan and bring to the boil. Add giblets if available, reduce heat and simmer for 1½ hours.

2 Check that the chicken is tender, allow to cool in the stock.

3 Remove chicken and strain stock for use in soups and sauces.

The chicken may be used in the following way:
  The legs and thighs can be used chopped in stuffings, sauces, chicken soups, pasta salads (pages 60-67) and chicken lasagne (page 79). The breasts may be sliced and served in a well flavoured sauce, e.g. lemon chicken with wholewheat spaghetti (page 78).

Note

To make chicken stock with remnants of a cooked bird use all the scraps and carcass of cooked chicken. Reduce the liquid to 2.4 l/4 pt.

Makes 10 cups/2 l/4 pt

CHICKEN BROTH

Chicken broth

Ingredients

1 tbsp/15 g/½ oz butter
1 onion, peeled and diced
3 leeks, washed
1 bouquet garni
1 bay leaf
2 stalks parsley
2½ cups/600 ml/1 pt chicken stock
⅔ cup/100 g/4 oz chopped cooked chicken
½ cup/75 g/3 oz vermicelli
2 tbsp chopped parsley

To prepare

1 Melt the butter in a saucepan and cook the onion over a low heat until transparent.

2 Prepare the leeks by removing the coarse outer leaves, trim off the coarse tops and then cut a cross down the centre of the leek, i.e. two lengthwise cuts to the white part. This enables the mud to be washed off easily under a cold running tap.

3 Add the leeks to the onion and stir well. Drop the bouquet garni, bay leaf and parsley stalks into the saucepan.

4 Pour the stock in and cook for 10 minutes after bringing to the boil. Simmer for the cooking time.

5 Taste for seasoning, add the cooked chicken and vermicelli. Simmer for a further 7 minutes then add the chopped parsley. Taste for seasoning before serving. Remove bouquet garni bay leaf and parsley stalk.

Serves 4

Ingredients
450-g/1-lb shin of beef
1 kg/2 lb beef and veal bones
2 onions, peeled and sliced
2 carrots, peeled and sliced
1 bouquet garni
1 bay leaf
6 crushed peppercorns
10 cups/2.4 l/4 pt water
Oven temperature 200°C/400°F/Gas 6.

To prepare

1 Slice the meat thinly and arrange in a roasting pan with the roughly chopped bones and vegetables. Place in a hot oven to brown.

2 After 30 minutes when the bones and meat are brown, drain off the fat and transfer the meat and bones into a large saucepan. Add the herbs and peppercorns with the water, to the bones and vegetables.

3 Bring to the boil, remove any scum with a slotted spoon and allow to simmer for 1½-2 hours. Strain when cool and allow any fat to solidify on the top. Use as required — any excess can be stored in the freezer for special dishes, such as consommé.

Brown stock can also be made in smaller quantities in the oven in a casserole when it is being used for long term cooking. To make in a pressure cooker follow manufacturers' instructions.

Makes 7½ cups/ 1¾ l/3 pt stock

Ingredients
2½ cups/600 ml/1 pt brown stock
salt and freshly ground pepper
2 egg whites with shells
¼ cup/50 g/2 oz lean minced (ground) beef
1 small leek
2 tbsp chopped parsley
2 tbsp dry sherry

To prepare

1 Make sure the brown stock (page 54) is as free of fat as possible. Season well.

2 Whisk the two egg whites until slightly frothy and mix with the minced beef. Mix with 1¼ cups/300 ml/½ pt cold stock.

3 Bring the remaining stock to the boil with the chopped leek and parsley. Turn the heat off.

4 Gradually add the whisked egg and beef mixture, stirring the stock to distribute the egg mixture evenly.

5 Add the egg shells after crushing them in a plastic bag.

6 Bring the mixture back to simmering point stirring while it is heating. Stop stirring when bubbles appear on the surface and allow the egg white to come to the surface.

7 Allow pan to simmer very slowly almost off the heat for about 10 minutes.

8 Arrange a sieve lined with muslin (cheesecloth) over another saucepan or bowl. Carefully pour the stock through making sure that the egg white mixture remains in one lump.

9 Allow the consommé to stand for a few minutes then add the sherry. Use as required.

Serves 4

CAPPELLETTI IN CONSOMME

Ingredients
5 cups/1.2 1/2 pts chicken broth or consommé
450 g/1 lb cappelletti
To garnish
1 tbsp freshly chopped parsley

To prepare

1 Bring the broth or consommé to the boil and drop the cappelletti into the boiling liquid.

2 Cook simmering briskly for about 15 minutes. Test the capelletti after 12 minutes and taste the liquid for seasoning.

3 Serve sprinkled with freshly chopped parsley.

Cappelletti or tortellini stuffed with beef or veal are better served in consommé and chicken stuffing is better complemented by a chicken broth.

Serves 4

TOMATO PASTA SOUP

Ingredients

1 onion, peeled and sliced
1 leek, washed and sliced
1 stalk celery
1 tbsp oil
1 tbsp/15 g/½ oz butter
1 tbsp flour
3¾ cups/900 ml/1½ pt stock
1½ cups/425 g/15 oz canned tomatoes
4 tomatoes, skinned and chopped
1 tbsp tomato purée
1 stalk parsley
1 tbsp chopped fresh or 1 tsp dried basil
1 bay leaf
salt and pepper
2 tbsp cream
½ cup/50 g/2 oz small pasta shapes

To prepare

1 Prepare the vegetables making sure that the leek is trimmed, cut with a cross and thoroughly washed before chopping. Remove the strings from the celery with a sharp knife and slice.

2 Heat the oil and butter in a large saucepan and toss the vegetables in the fat over a low heat for 4 minutes.

3 Sprinkle with flour and mix well before adding the stock and tomatoes. Mix well with a wooden spoon before adding the herbs and seasoning. Bring to the boil and simmer for 35 minutes. Allow the soup to cool slightly before sieving or blending.

4 Return to the saucepan, taste for seasoning, bring to the boil and add the small pasta shapes. Cook by simmering for a further 5 minutes or until pasta is cooked. Stir in the cream and serve.

Serves 4

MINESTRONE SOUP

Ingredients

Ingredients
1 cup/225 g/8 oz dried white haricot (navy) beans
5 cups/1.2 l/2 pt water
salt and pepper
⅔ cup/100 g/4 oz bacon or salt pork
2 tbsp oil
2 onions, peeled and diced
2 carrots, scraped and diced
2-3 stalks celery, washed
1 potato, peeled and diced
1 clove garlic, crushed
1 bouquet garni
1 bay leaf
1 stalk parsley
3-4 leaves chopped or 1 tsp dried basil
1½ cups/425 g/15 oz canned tomatoes
1 tbsp tomato purée
⅔ cup/50 g/4 oz small pasta shapes
3 cups/225 g/8 oz green cabbage, washed and shredded
½ cup/50 g/2 oz frozen peas

To garnish

To garnish
2 tbsp freshly chopped parsley
⅓ cup/50 g/2 oz grated parmesan cheese

To prepare

1 Soak the haricot beans in cold water for at least 8 hours. Drain and place in a large saucepan with 2½ cups/ 1.2 l/2 pt cold water. Bring to the boil, add 1 tsp salt, boil fast for 10 minutes, then allow to simmer gently for another 30 minutes.

2 Dice the bacon or salt pork if using meat and allow to cook in a frying pan for 2-3 minutes. Add diced vegetables, onions and carrots, turning for a few minutes over a low heat.

3 Remove strings from celery with a sharp knife and slice into neat pieces. Add to the vegetables with the potato.

4 Add the vegetables to the haricot beans with a further 2½ cups/600 ml/1 pt water or stock depending on whether the liquid has reduced.

5 Add herbs and seasonings. After the soup has been simmering for 15 minutes add the canned tomatoes and purée, stir well to mix.

6 After a further 15 minutes add green beans and pasta.

7 Allow to simmer for a further 5 minutes and then add cabbage and peas. When the pasta is cooked, taste for seasoning and remove the bouquet garni, bay leaf and parsley stalk. Serve each bowl sprinkled with chopped parsley and cheese.

Note

Vegetables can be varied according to availability and preference and more garlic and Italian sausage may be added to taste.

Minestrone may also be served garnished with a spoonful of Genoese Pesto Sauce (page 48) served on top in place of Parmesan. This is a treat for lovers of garlic.

Serves 4-6

SALADS

Salads made with cold pasta are great party favourites. The many varieties of pasta blend so well with meat, fish and vegetables that endless variations on the salad theme can be made.

Cooked pasta blends well with mayonnaise and other salad dressings and any left-over pasta comes in useful for another meal. It is often convenient to cook extra pasta and store it in the freezer for this purpose.

The interesting shapes and colours of different pastas are most appealing in simple cold dishes.

Chicken pasta avocado salad

PRAWNS (SHRIMP) AND PASTA SALAD

Ingredients

1⅓ cups/225 g/8 oz cooked pasta shells

1¼ cups/300 ml/½ pt mayonnaise (page 49)

2 tsp tomato purée

2-3 drops Tabasco sauce

juice of ½ lemon

¾ cup/100 g/4 oz cooked peeled prawns (shrimps)

½ lettuce, washed

1 bunch watercress, washed

To garnish

large prawns (shrimps) in shells (optional)

To prepare

1 Place the cooked pasta shells in a bowl.

2 Mix the mayonnaise with the tomato purée and Tabasco sauce.

3 Sprinkle the lemon juice over the prawns.

4 Arrange the lettuce and watercress sprigs on the bottom of and around a salad bowl.

5 Add the mayonnaise to the pasta shells with the prawns and mix well.

6 Pile the prawns and pasta in the centre of the salad bowl lined with lettuce and watercress sprigs. Garnish with large prawns.

Serves 4

Ingredients
2 stalks celery, washed
1 eating apple, peeled
juice of 1 lemon
1⅓ cups/225 g/8 oz cooked pasta wheels
⅝ cup/150 ml/¼ pt mayonnaise (page 49)
1 small lettuce
8 slices salami
To garnish
2 tomatoes
Celery leaves

To prepare

1 Remove the strings from the celery stalks with a sharp knife and cut into thin slices. Dice the eating apple and mix with the celery.

2 Sprinkle the lemon juice on the celery and apple and arrange on the bottom of a dish lined with lettuce.

3 Mix the pasta wheels with the mayonnaise, arrange on top of the apples and celery.

4 Roll up slices of salami and arrange in a wheel patter on the pasta wheels.

5 Garnish with tomato wedges and some celery leaves in the centre.

Serves 4

WHOLEFOOD PASTA SALAD

Ingredients

2 cups/225 g/8 oz wholewheat pasta spirals

juice of 1 lemon

⅝ cup/150 ml/¼ pt natural yoghurt

½ tsp cumin

½ clove garlic, crushed

salt and freshly ground pepper

1 small lettuce, washed

1 bunch watercress, washed

1 tbsp bran

Wholefood pasta salad

To prepare

1 Cook the spirals for 10-12 minutes, drain and rinse in cold water. Allow to drain well in a colander.

2 Put the yoghurt into a bowl and mix with the cumin, crushed garlic and seasoning. Add a few drops of lemon juice.

3 Toss the pasta in the yoghurt dressing.

4 Arrange the drained lettuce and watercress in a salad bowl, sprinkle with lemon juice. Arrange the pasta in the centre of the bowl and sprinkle with the bran.

Cucumber and tomatoes can be added.

Serves 4

CHICKEN AVOCADO PASTA SALAD

Ingredients

1⅓ cups/225 g/8 oz cooked pasta

6 spring (green) onions, washed

⅝ cup/150 ml/¼ pt mayonnaise (page 49)

2 ripe avocados

1⅓ cups/225 g/8 oz cooked chicken, chopped

salt and freshly ground pepper

2 tomatoes, skinned and sliced

1 red pepper, seeded

parsley or watercress (optional)

To prepare

1 Place the cooked pasta in a bowl. Chop the spring onions finely and add to the pasta with the mayonnaise.

2 Remove the skins from the avocados, cut in half and remove the stones. Cut 8 thin slices for garnish and chop the remainder. Add to the pasta and mayonnaise mixture with the cooked chicken.

3 Season well and add a few drops of lemon juice. Place the sliced avocado in the remaining lemon juice.

4 Arrange the salad in a bowl which has been lined with sliced tomatoes.

5 Decorate with slices of blanched pepper and the sliced avocados. Arrange parsley or watercress around the dish.

If preparing in advance leave the avocados in lemon juice until just before serving.

Any wholewheat pasta shape may be used such as shells, spirals or short cut macaroni.

Serves 4

TORTELLINI COLESLAW

Ingredients

1⅓ cups/225 g/8 oz stuffed tortellini, cooked

3 tbsp olive oil

1 tbsp white wine vinegar

1 tsp French mustard

salt and freshly ground pepper

Coleslaw

½ cabbage (approx 450 g/1 lb)

1 carrot, scraped and grated

2 spring (green) onions, washed and chopped

2 tbsp/25 g/1 oz raisins

2 stalks celery, washed

⅝ cup/150 ml/¼ pt mayonnaise

To garnish

Black olives

To prepare

1 Place the cooked tortellini (after rinsing in cold water and draining) in a bowl.

2 Mix the dressing by placing the oil, vinegar, mustard and seasoning in a screw-top jar. Shake well and pour over the pasta.

3 Make the coleslaw by washing, draining and shredding the cabbage. Mix in a separate bowl with the grated carrot and raisins.

4 After washing the celery remove the strings with a sharp knife and then chop into thin slices, add to the cabbage and season well.

5 Mix the mayonnaise into the vegetable mixture.

6 Arrange rows of coleslaw with alternating rows of tortellini for a pretty and delicious salad.

Serves 4-6

SALADS

RAVIOLI IN TOMATO DRESSING

Ingredients

1⅓ cups/225 g/8 oz cooked ravioli

Tomato dressing

1½ cups/450 g/1 lb tomatoes, skinned and chopped

1 tbsp fresh basil leaves or parsley

1 tsp lemon juice

salt and freshly ground pepper

4 tbsp olive oil

1 clove garlic, crushed

To prepare

1 Make up the dressing in a jar with a screw-top as can be done for French dressing.

2 Chop the basil or parsley finely and add all ingredients to the jar, shake vigorously and leave to stand for at least half an hour in the refrigerator before using.

3 Shake well and coat the cooked cold ravioli.

This recipe can be used with any variety of stuffed pasta and is attractive on a buffet table.

MAIN DISHES

Chilli con carne with pasta shells

SHOULDER OF VEAL WITH MUSHROOMS AND SPINACH FETTUCINI

Ingredients

1½ kg/3-3½ lb boned rolled shoulder of veal

1 tbsp oil

1 small onion, peeled and sliced

salt and freshly ground pepper

4 tbsp dry white wine

2½ cups/600 ml/1 pt bechamel sauce (page 38)

4 cups/225 g/8 oz mushrooms, washed and sliced

1 tbsp freshly chopped parsley

675 g/1½ lb fresh spinach fettucini

½ tsp oil

2 tbsp/25 g/1 oz butter

a little freshly grated nutmeg

Oven temperature 200°C/400°F/Gas 6.

To prepare

1 Place the boned rolled shoulder in a roasting pan. Pour the oil on top, scatter the sliced onions on top and season well. Pour on the wine.

2 Cook in the oven for 1½ hours turning the temperature down for the last hour to 180°C/350°F/Gas 4.

4 Make up the bechamel sauce, season well and add mushrooms, cook for 5 minutes.

5 Cook the fettucini or pasta of your choice in boiling salted water with a few drops of oil added. Fresh fettucini will take 2 minutes. Drain and toss in butter, arrange in a warm serving dish.

6 Slice the meat after allowing to stand for 10 minutes. Arrange sliced meat on the pasta and keep warm.

7 Drain the fat from the roasting pan, add 4 tbsp water, boil, then add meat juices to the mushroom sauce and stir well. Coat the sliced veal, serve piping hot.

Serves 4

STUFFED PORK CHOPS WITH PASTA BOWS

Ingredients

1 tbsp breadcrumbs

1 tbsp oil

1 small onion, peeled

½ tsp dried or 1 tsp chopped fresh sage

1 cup/50 g/2 oz mushrooms, washed and chopped

1 tsp freshly chopped parsley

½ tsp grated lemon rind

salt and freshly ground pepper

4 thick pork chops

2 cups/450 ml/¾ pt pomodoro sauce (page 43)

2 cups/225 g/8 oz pasta bows

2 tbsp/25 g/1 oz butter

freshly grated nutmeg

To garnish

1 bunch watercress

Oven temperature 180°C/350°F/Gas 4.

To prepare

1 Put fresh white breadcrumbs in a small mixing bowl.

2 Heat the oil and cook the finely diced onion over a low heat for 4 minutes, add finely chopped mushrooms and cook for a further 2 minutes.

3 Add sage, parsley, lemon rind, salt and pepper to the breadcrumbs. Tip the onion and mushrooms into the bowl and mix well.

4 Cut a slit in the chop at the fat end. Stuff the slit with the onion and mushroom stuffing. Place the chops under the grill (broiler) for 4 minutes each side. Dry on kitchen paper to remove excess fat.

5 Arrange the chops in an ovenproof dish, pour over the tomato sauce, cover with foil and bake for 25 minutes.

6 Cook the pasta bows for about 10 minutes, drain and toss in melted butter. Add a shake of pepper and nutmeg. Serve the bows and chops garnished with watercress.

Serves 4

MEDITERRANEAN BEEF CASSEROLE

Ingredients

675 g/1½ lb lean braising steak
2 tbsp seasoned flour
4 tbsp oil
2 rashers (2 strips) bacon
2 onions, peeled and diced
2 cloves garlic, crushed
1 leek, washed
2 stalks celery, washed
2 red peppers, seeded and diced
1½ cups/425 g/15 oz canned tomatoes
1¼ cups/300 ml/½ pt stock or water
4 tbsp red wine
salt and freshly ground black pepper
1-2 bay leaves
1 bouquet garni
sprig of fresh or 1 tsp dried thyme
1¾ cups whole/2 cups sliced/100 g/4 oz mushrooms
3 cups/350 g/12 oz penne pasta
1 tbsp/15 g/½ oz butter
pinch of nutmeg

To garnish

1 tbsp freshly chopped parsley (optional)
Oven temperature 180°C/350°F/Gas 4

To prepare

1 Trim the meat to remove excess fat or gristle, cut into small 1½-cm (½-in) cubes. Toss the cubes in seasoned flour.

2 Heat half the oil in a frying pan on a high heat, turn down a little and fry the meat on all sides to seal. Drain on to a plate and leave the meat juices in the frying pan.

3 Put the remaining oil in an ovenproof casserole and cook the onion over a low heat for about 3 minutes. Add crushed garlic.

4 Remove the strings from the celery with a sharp knife and then cut into neat slices. Add to the onions.

5 Add the carrot and diced peppers, toss all vegetables in the oil over a low heat for 2 minutes. Add the meat and the tomatoes to the casserole.

6 Pour the stock into the frying pan and mix with the meat juices and the red wine over a low heat. Pour over the meat and vegetables. Add the herbs.

7 Bring to the boil and cook in the oven for 1 hour or until meat is tender. Add mushrooms either sliced or whole half way through the cooking time. The casserole may be cooked on top of the cooker but must only simmer gently for about 45 minutes.

8 Cook the pasta in boiling salted water with a few drops of oil added for approximately 12 minutes. Drain and toss in a little melted butter with a shake of pepper and nutmeg.

9 Serve with the casserole which may be garnished with chopped parsley.

This is an excellent dish to prepare in advance as the flavour improves when the dish is re-heated.

Serves 4

LAMB IN DILL SAUCE WITH TAGLIOLINI

Ingredients

4 tbsp oil

1 medium onion, peeled and diced

450 g/1 lb minced (ground) lamb or veal

2 tbsp fresh white breadcrumbs

salt and freshly ground pepper

1 egg, beaten

2 tsp dried dill

1 tbsp chopped parsley

½ tsp Worcester sauce

juice of 1 lemon

2 egg yolks

1¼ cups/300 ml/½ pt sour cream

1 tbsp freshly chopped or 2 tsp dried dill

450 g/1 lb fresh tagliolini verdi

To garnish

freshly chopped dill or parsley

To prepare

1 Heat half the oil in a frying pan and cook the onion over a low heat until soft and transparent. Drain from the pan with a slotted spoon and reserve the remaining oil. Put the onions in a mixing bowl and allow to cool.

2 Add the minced lamb or veal to onions with the breadcrumbs, seasoning, beaten egg and Worcester sauce.

3 Mix well and with floured hands shape the mixture into balls 2½ cm (1 in) in diameter. Roll them lightly in seasoned flour.

4 Add the remaining oil to the pan and brown the meatballs over a high heat for about 1 minute each side. Reduce heat and continue cooking for about 8 minutes.

5 Cook the fresh green tagliolini or fettucini for 2-3 minutes in boiling salted water with a few drops of oil. Drain the pasta and toss in a little melted butter with a shake of nutmeg. Arrange meatballs on the pasta and keep warm for a few minutes until the sauce is made.

6 To make the sauce, mix the egg yolks with a little cream and then add the dill.

7 Add the remaining cream to the juices in the pan in which the meat was fried. Stir well, add some of the warm cream to the egg and return to the pan. Add lemon juice and warm through. Pour the warmed sauce onto the meatballs, sprinkle with fresh dill or parsley and serve immediately. Do not boil the sauce if you are re-heating it.

Serves 4

LEMON CHICKEN WITH WHOLEWHEAT SPAGHETTI

Ingredients

4 thick slices cooked chicken

1¼ cups/300 ml/½ pt bechamel sauce (page 38)

2 tsp lime juice

juice of ½ lemon

1½ cups/175 g/6 oz wholewheat spaghetti

oil

To garnish

lemon wedges

sprigs of parsley

To prepare

1 Heat the chicken in the bechamel sauce which has the lime and lemon juice added. The sauce can be made with chicken stock and chicken breasts (page 52).

2 Cook the pasta 2-3 minutes if fresh (12 minutes if dried) in boiling salted water with a few drops of oil added. Drain and toss in a little butter. Serve with the chicken in sauce.

Garnish with sprigs of parsley and lemon wedges.

Serves 2

CHICKEN AND MUSHROOM LASAGNE

Lemon chicken with wholewheat spaghetti

Ingredients
1 onion, peeled and diced
2 tbsp/25 g/1 oz butter
2 cups/100 g/4 oz mushrooms, washed and sliced
2 cups/350 g/12 oz cooked chicken, diced
2 tbsp fresh breadcrumbs
2½ cups/600 ml/1 pt bechamel sauce (page 38)
3 tbsp/25 g/1 oz grated parmesan cheese
9 sheets lasagne
salt and freshly ground white pepper
Oven temperature 180°C/350°F/Gas 4

To prepare

1 Cook the onion in the butter over a low heat for about 3 minutes. Add the mushrooms and cook for a further 2 minutes.

2 Add the chicken to the mushroom and onions, season well and mix with chopped parsley.

3 Make up the bechamel sauce, season well.

4 Place about 4 tbsp sauce in the bottom of an ovenproof dish. Cover with one third of the chicken mixture. Place sheets of 'non-cook' lasagne on top to cover. If using fresh it can be cooked in boiling water for 3 minutes.

5 Place a further 4 tbsp sauce on top of the lasagne and a further third of the chicken mixture. Continue with third layer of lasagne, top with remaining bechamel sauce.

6 Mix the fresh crumbs with the cheese and sprinkle on top. Bake in the oven for 25 minutes until golden brown.

Serves 4-6

SPAGHETTI WITH CHICKEN LIVERS

Ingredients

450 g/1 lb chicken livers, diced

1 red pepper, seeded

1 clove garlic, crushed

4 tbsp/50 g/2 oz butter

salt and freshly ground pepper

4 tomatoes, skinned and chopped

2 basil leaves, chopped

450 g/1 lb spaghetti

oil

freshly chopped parsley (optional)

To prepare

1 Prepare the chicken livers by cutting into small pieces.

2 Cut and dice the pepper finely. Blanch it for 2 minutes in water that has just boiled and drain. Crush the garlic.

3 Melt the butter in a frying pan and simmer the garlic and pepper for 5 minutes.

4 Add the chicken livers and stir round mixing with the pepper. Cook for 5-6 minutes on a low heat. Add the tomatoes, basil and seasoning.

5 While the sauce is simmering cook the spaghetti in boiling salted water with a few drops of oil. Drain and mix well with the chicken liver sauce. Each portion can be garnished with some freshly chopped parsley.

Serves 4

ORANGE LIVER PASTA

Ingredients
450 g/1 lb calves liver
1 tbsp flour
salt and freshly ground pepper
1 onion, skinned and diced
4 tbsp/50 g/2 oz butter
1 tbsp oil
1 orange
1 tbsp sherry
⅝ cup/150 ml/¼ pt beef stock
4 large tomatoes, skinned and chopped
½ lb/225 g/8 oz tagliatelli
1 tbsp/15 g/½ oz butter
pinch of nutmeg
To garnish
4 orange slices
1 tbsp chopped parsley

To prepare

1 Cut the liver into thin strips about 1 cm (½ in) thick and 3½ cm (1½ in) in length. Dip in the flour seasoned with salt and pepper.

2 Heat the butter and oil, turn heat to low and allow the onion to cook without browning for 3 minutes. Remove with a slotted spoon to a plate.

3 Turn the heat up slightly and stir-fry the strips of liver for 3-4 minutes. Care must be taken that the liver is only lightly brown or it will toughen.

4 Grate the rind from the orange, cut in half and remove 4 thin slices for garnish. Squeeze the juice from the remaining orange.

5 Add the sherry, orange juice, stock orange rind to the liver with the onions and simmer gently for 5 minutes. Finally add the chopped tomatoes and simmer for a further 8 minutes, after stirring to mix ingredients.

6 Cook the fresh tagliatelli in boiling salted water for 2 minutes to which a little oil has been added. Drain well and toss in a little melted butter with a shake of grated nutmeg and pepper. Arrange on warm plates or serving platter with orange liver on top. Garnish with a twist of orange and chopped parsley.

Serves 4

SAUSAGE SAVORY BAKE WITH TAGLIATELLI

Ingredients
8 pork sausages
8 slices bacon
1¼ cups/300 ml/½ pt tomato sauce (page 42)
½ lb/225 g/8 oz tagliatelli
salt and freshly ground pepper
oil
1 tbsp/15 g/½ oz butter
pinch of nutmeg
To garnish
freshly chopped parsley
Oven temperature 180°C/350°F/Gas 4

To prepare

1 Prick the sausages once and wrap one slice of bacon around each sausage. Place under a hot grill (broiler) for about 2 minutes each side. Drain on kitchen paper.

2 Arrange in an ovenproof dish and pour the tomato sauce over the sausages. Bake in the oven for 20 minutes.

3 Cook fresh tagliatelli for 2 minutes (or dried for 7) in boiling salted water with a few drops of oil. Drain into a colander and toss in a little melted butter with a shake of pepper and nutmeg.

4 Arrange the pasta around the sausages or on individual heated plates as preferred. Sprinkle with freshly chopped parsley.

Serves 4

SPAGHETTI CARBONARA

Ingredients

450 g/1 lb spaghetti

salt and freshly ground pepper

½ tsp oil

1 onion, peeled and finely sliced

5 slices of back bacon

2 cups/100 g/4 oz mushrooms, washed and sliced

4 tbsp/50 g/2 oz butter

5 eggs, beaten

⅓ cup/50 g/2 oz parmesan cheese

1 tbsp freshly chopped parsley

To prepare

1 Cook the spaghetti in a large saucepan of boiling salted water with a few drops oil added, for 12 minutes. Drain well.

2 Meanwhile prepare the other ingredients, slice the onion, and dice the bacon. Wash and slice the mushrooms.

3 Melt half the butter in a large pan and cook the onion and bacon for 5 minutes over a low heat. Add the mushrooms and cook for a further 3 minutes.

4 Toss the drained spaghetti in the other half of the melted butter over a medium heat for a few seconds. Season with pepper, add cheese.

5 Toss the spaghetti into the pan with the onion, bacon and mushrooms and mix well. Add the seasoned beaten egg and stir vigorously into the mixture. Cook over the heat for a few minutes until thick and creamy.

6 Serve on warmed plates or serving dish sprinkled with chopped parsley.

Serves 4

MACARONI CHEESE WITH BACON AND TOMATO

Ingredients

1 cup/175 g/6 oz short cut macaroni

salt and freshly ground pepper

½ tsp oil

1 tbsp/25 g/1 oz butter

2½ cups/600 ml/1 pt mornay sauce (page 38)

½ cup/50 g/2 oz grated cheese

1 tbsp fresh breadcrumbs

4 slices of back bacon

2 tomatoes, sliced

Oven temperature 200°C/400°F/Gas 6

To prepare

1 Cook the macaroni for 7 minutes in boiling salted water to which a few drops of oil have been added. Drain well.

2 Butter an ovenproof dish and prepare the sauce.

3 Mix the macaroni with the sauce and pour into the dish.

4 Sprinkle with grated cheese mixed with fresh breadcrumbs.

5 Arrange the bacon slices on top of the macaroni alternately with tomato slices. Cook for 15-20 minutes until bacon is cooked.

Serves 4

CHILLI PASTA

Ingredients
2 tbsp oil
2 cloves garlic, crushed
450 g/1 lb lean minced (ground) beef
2 small onions, peeled
1 red pepper, seeded
1 green pepper, seeded
1 small chilli pepper
1½ cups/425 g/15 oz canned tomatoes
¼ tsp chilli powder
⅝ cup/150 ml/¼ pt beef stock
1 small can kidney beans or ½ cup/100 g/4 oz dried beans, soaked and cooked
2 cups/350 g/12 oz pasta shells, cooked
salt and freshly ground pepper
2 tbsp/25 g/1 oz butter
shake of grated nutmeg

To prepare

1 Heat the oil in a pan, add the crushed garlic and the meat, turn over with a fork until the meat is brown and separated into particles. Break down lumps with a fork. Add the diced onion and continue cooking over a low heat until the onions are slightly transparent.

2 Cut the peppers into bite-size strips and add to the meat.

3 Seed the chilli pepper taking care the seeds do not touch the skin or eyes. Try to use thin rubber gloves as contact with chilli is quite painful. Dice into small pieces and add to the meat mixture which is still cooking slowly over a low heat.

4 Add the canned tomatoes, chilli powder and beef stock and bring to the boil, then simmer for 45 minutes. Add canned beans 15 minutes before serving. Dried beans must be soaked and boiled for 30 minutes before being added to the chilli for 30 minutes of cooking time. Taste for seasoning and add salt and pepper if necessary.

5 Serve with a bowl of cooked hot pasta which has been tossed in butter with a shake of nutmeg.

Serves 4

BAKED HAM AND BROCCOLI

Ingredients
8 slices of cooked ham
8 florets of fresh or frozen broccoli
2½ cups/600 ml/1 pt mornay sauce (page 38)
1 tsp dried mustard
½ cup/50 g/2 oz grated cheese
2 cups/350 g/12 oz cooked pasta shapes
salt and freshly ground pepper
shake of grated or 1 tsp ground nutmeg
Oven temperature 180°C/350°F/Gas 4

To prepare

1 Lay out slices of ham on a board.

2 Wash and drain fresh broccoli. If using frozen place in boiling water for 3 minutes, drain well.

3 Roll the broccoli florets in the ham neatly.

4 To make up the mornay sauce, grated cheddar may be used or a mixture with parmesan cheese. Add dried mustard and mix well.

5 Butter an ovenproof dish, arrange the pasta on the bottom, season with a shake of pepper and nutmeg. Arrange the filled ham on top.

6 Pour over the sauce and finish with sprinkled grated cheese. Cook for 20 minutes or until cheese is golden on top.

Serves 4

ORIENTAL STIR-FRY VEGETABLES WITH NOODLES

Ingredients
4 tbsp olive oil
1 onion, peeled
1 red pepper, seeded
1 green pepper, seeded
1 small chilli pepper, seeded
1 clove garlic, crushed
3 cups/175 g/6 oz mushrooms, washed and sliced
1 small cauliflower
2 courgettes (zucchini), washed
1⅓ cups/100 g/4 oz French beans
2 cups/350 g/12 oz egg noodles
½ tsp oil
salt and freshly ground pepper
2 tbsp soy sauce

To prepare

1 Prepare the vegetables by thinly slicing the onions and the peppers, dice the chilli finely, crush the garlic and slice the mushrooms. Divide the cauliflower into small florets and slice the courgettes and the beans.

2 Heat the oil in a large casserole or wok, throw in the onions and other vegetables a few at a time and stir-fry for about 5 minutes turning the vegetables over to obtain an even distribution of heat.

3 Stir in the seasoning and soy sauce.

4 Cook the noodles in boiling salted water for about 6 minutes, drain well and toss in a little butter. Serve with the vegetables.

Serves 4

LOSHKEN PUDDING

Ingredients

½ lb/225 g/8 oz egg vermicelli
1 tsp salt
½ tsp oil
½ cup/50 g/2 oz chopped candied fruit peel
½ cup/50 g/2 oz almond slivers
4 tbsp/50 g/2 oz butter
¼ tsp ground cinnamon
¼ tsp allspice
¼ cup/50 g/2 oz sugar
2 eggs, beaten
⅝ cup/150 ml/¼ pt cream

To decorate

20 halved almonds

Oven temperature 180°C/350°F/Gas 4

To prepare

1 Cook the vermicelli in a large saucepan of boiling water to which the salt and oil have been added. Test after 2 minutes. If the vermicelli is almost cooked, drain and return to the saucepan.

2 Add the candied peel, almond slivers, and the butter cut into small knobs. Mix well.

3 Sprinkle the spices over the mixture.

4 Mix the sugar with the beaten egg and add to the pasta mixture. Lastly stir in the cream.

5 Turn into a buttered pie dish and bake for 10 minutes.

6 Remove from the oven after 10 minutes and decorate with 'almond flowers' ie make petals with the halved almonds. Return to the oven for a further 8-10 minutes until golden.

Serves 4

APRICOT MACARONI PUDDING

Ingredients
generous ½ cup/75 g/3 oz short cut macaroni
2 tbsp/25 g/1 oz butter
425-g/15-oz can apricots
1¼/300 ml/½ pt evaporated milk
1 tbsp cornflour (cornstarch)
¼ cup/50 g/2 oz sugar
1 tbsp brown sugar
Oven temperature 180°C/350°F/Gas 4

To prepare

1 Cook the macaroni in boiling salted water for 5 minutes, drain and return to the saucepan.

2 Butter an ovenproof dish then add the remaining butter to the macaroni. Turn half the buttered macaroni into the dish.

3 Drain the can of apricots and mix the juice with the cornflour. Arrange half the apricots on top of the macaroni.

4 Heat the cornflour and juice. Add the hot mixture to the cold evaporated milk and sugar and return the mixture to a low heat for a few minutes. Pour half the liquid over the macaroni and apricots.

5 Place the remaining macaroni on top of the apricots and pour on the remaining sauce.

6 Arrange the other apricots on top of the pudding and sprinkle with brown sugar. Bake for 35 minutes or until macaroni is cooked.

Serves 4-6

INTRODUCTION

Wholewheat pepper and caper pizza

The pizza originated in Naples, an invention of Neapolitan bakers for the poverty-stricken inhabitants of the back streets of the city, to make a little food stretch a long way. Because it is still a cheap and cheerful way to eat, the pizza has become even more popular in other countries than it is in Italy and there are pizza restaurants all over the world.

The Neapolitan pizza is made with fresh tomatoes, oregano, anchovy fillets, mozzarella cheese and olive oil. There are now countless toppings for pizzas and making them at home is an excellent way of utilizing fresh vegetables, meats and cheese to add variety to family meals.

Salami, chicken, bacon, smoked hams and spicy sausages can all be used as toppings with different cheeses on a tomato base.

Fish pizzas can be flavoured with anchovies, clams, mussels, prawns, shrimps, and tuna fish on tomatoes and herbs.

Pizzas are also a great boon to vegetarians as a tomato base is ideal with mushrooms, green, red or yellow peppers, aubergines (eggplant), artichoke hearts, sweetcorn (corn), herbs, black or green olives with or without cheese according to preference.

Professional pizza chefs hurl the dough in the air to achieve the correct thickness but at home the dough can be rolled and moulded without this particular technique. The authentic pizza texture imparted by a brick-built pizza oven cannot be recreated exactly at home. Homemade pizzas are therefore bound to be slightly different, but they are still very good and you can be sure of delicious toppings. The deep pan pizza is much easier to copy at home with the aid of a flan ring or sandwich cake tin.

Bake your own pizzas to suit your family's tastes and you will discover, as have the Neapolitan bakers, that a little does indeed go a long way. Small children, teenagers and adults are enthusiastic pizza-eaters and pizzas are therefore always popular. A glass of wine and a pizza are really only the equivalents of a beer and a sandwich, but they always seem more exciting.

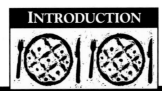
Making bread dough for pizzas is straightforward providing the cook who is not familiar with yeast cookery keeps the following notes in mind when using the recipes. Enough time must be allowed for the dough to prove, but during this time it requires no attention and other work may be done.

FLOUR

Strong white flour is best for bread doughs as it has a high gluten content which helps to give the texture and volume associated with bread doughs. As a warm atmosphere suits yeast particularly well, it is a good idea to sieve flour into a slightly warmed bowl.

Many people prefer whole grain flours today and enjoy wholewheat pizzas. It must be noted that a mixture using only wholewheat flour will be fairly solid to eat but this is a matter of for individual taste. A mixture of strong white flour and wholewheat gives a more digestible pizza.

YEAST

is a living organism which is used as a raising agent in bread doughs. Yeast feeds on sugars and multiplies in warm moist conditions releasing carbon dioxide which expands when heated to give dough its characteristic spongy texture. However yeast can also be killed by excessive heat and it is essential that the yeast mixture be the correct temperature around 43°C/110°F. Yeast wakes up gradually — do not be too impatient.

SALT

contributes to the flavour of the dough but it can also kill yeast cells. Only use the recommended amounts and do not allow the salt to come into direct contact with the yeast. The salt should be sieved or mixed with the flour. The proportion is usually 2 tsp to each 4½ cups/450 g/1 lb flour used.

SUGAR

if creamed with yeast can kill it; therefore it is essential not to add more than the amounts given in the recipes. Sugar added to the measured liquid and dissolved will be enough to activate the yeast without overpowering it.

LIQUIDS

used in yeast mixtures are either milk or water or a combination of the two. It is most important for the liquid to be the correct temperature. If it is warmer than 43°C/110°F it will destroy yeast cells. Try putting a finger in the water; if it feels warm, cool it slightly. Most beginners make the liquid too hot.

It is also important to measure liquids and put in less than the recipe states as more liquid can always be added but too much cannot be removed. Add the last of it carefully to obtain a slightly sticky but not wet dough. The mixture will firm to an elastic consistency as it is kneaded. It is this process which develops the gluten in the flour to give the texture.

RISING TIMES

It is very difficult to give the precise time required for activating yeast — it all depends on the ambient temperature. In cold surroundings yeast grows but only slowly.

In a warm place in front of a central heating radiator or warm cupboard it will take about an hour. At room temperature dough can take up to 2 hours to rise. In a cool room it will rise in about 5 hours and in a refrigerator in about 12 hours.

These rising times are useful to remember as the process can be organized around other activities.

ASSEMBLING INGREDIENTS FOR DOUGH

1 Measure all ingredients accurately. Sieve flour.

2 On the right of the board there is fresh yeast which can be bought from some bakers, delicatessens and health food shops.

3 On the left of the board the jug contains dried yeast mixed with liquid being left to ferment for 15 minutes.

ADDING THE YEAST MIXTURE TO THE FLOUR

Make a well in the centre of the flour, add oil and cover with a little flour. Pour in the yeast liquid and the remaining liquid.

MIXING THE DOUGH

Use a palette knife or plastic spatula to mix the dough until all the liquid has been absorbed to make a firm but pliable dough. Add liquid carefully at the end to prevent the dough becoming too sticky. If you add too much liquid, you will have to work in more flour which spoils the dough's consistency.

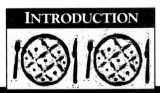
MAKING PIZZA DOUGH

KNEADING THE DOUGH

When the dough is mixed turn onto a floured board and knead vigorously for 10 minutes. The kneading motion is done by pushing with the heel of the hand and turning the dough over continuously until it is smooth.

PROVING THE DOUGH

Place in a bowl which has been lightly floured or in an oiled plastic bag. If using a bowl, cover with plastic wrap or place inside a plastic bag or cover with a clean tea towel. This careful covering of the dough is to stop cooling air currents from interfering with the rising processs. The dough (right) has risen and the covering just removed. Proving at this stage will take approximately an hour in a warm room, longer if the room is cool.

KNOCKING BACK (PUNCHING DOWN) THE RISEN DOUGH

Turn the risen dough onto a floured board and knead again until the pockets of gas which are now unevenly distributed are knocked out (punched down). The dough is now smooth, firm and elastic.

For speed, many recipes shape the pizzas at this stage but for a really delicious home-made pizza use the Pizza Dough 2 recipe. The second rising develops the real texture and the extra time is worthwhile.

PIZZA DOUGH

PIZZA DOUGH 1

Ingredients

1 tbsp/15 g/½ oz fresh or 2 tsp dried yeast
½ cup/115 ml/4 fl oz slightly warmed water
1 tsp sugar
4½ cups/450 g/1 lb strong plain flour
1 tsp salt
1 tbsp oil

To prepare

1 Blend fresh yeast with a little of the measured water which has the sugar dissolved in it. For dried yeast dissolve 1 tsp sugar in one third of the measured water, sprinkle the yeast onto the water and whisk. Leave to stand for 10-15 minutes until frothy.

2 Sieve the flour and salt into a bowl and make a well in the centre, add the oil, sprinkle over with a little flour.

3 Add the yeast liquid and most of the remaining water and mix well until the dough starts to leave the side of the bowl. If it seems too stiff add the remaining liquid slowly.

4 Turn onto a lightly floured board and knead well for about 10 minutes. When the dough is elastic and smooth place in a floured bowl and cover with a tea towel or plastic wrap. Alternatively leave it to rise in an oiled plastic bag until it has doubled in size. This will take approximately an hour in a warm kitchen.

5 The dough can then be knocked back (punched down) and shaped for pizzas.

The dough with two risings in my opinion gives the better home-made pizza.

Makes 2 × 30-cm (12-in) pizzas or 3 × 20-cm (8-in) pizzas

PIZZA DOUGH 2

Ingredients

4½ cups/1.4 kg/3 lb flour
1 tbsp/30 g/1 oz salt
4 tbsp/50 g/2 oz fresh or 2 tbsp/25 g/1 oz dried yeast
2¼ cups/500 ml/18 fl oz water
½ cup/125 ml/4 fl oz milk
2 tbsp oil

To prepare

1 Sieve the flour into a large bowl and make a well in the centre.

2 Add the yeast by crumbling into the centre of the well.

3 Make sure that the water and milk are just body temperature and pour most of the mixture into the well with the yeast.

4 Dissolve the salt in a little of the remaining liquid. Add oil. Pour them into mixture.

5 Knead well for about 10 minutes by hand. Place back in the bowl or in an oiled large plastic bag.

6 Allow to stand in a warm kitchen for about an hour or until the dough has doubled in size.

7 Knock back (punch down) the dough by kneading well with the heel of the hand.

8 Replace the dough in the bowl or bag and allow to rise again for a further hour.

Makes 4 × 30-cm (12-in) oblong or round pizzas

WHOLEWHEAT PIZZA DOUGH

Ingredients

1 tbsp/15 g/½ oz fresh or 3 level tsp dried yeast

⅝ cup/150 ml/¼ pt slightly warmed water

1 tsp sugar

2¼ cups/225 g/8 oz wholewheat flour

2¼ cups/225 g/8 oz plain flour

1 tsp salt

1 tbsp oil

To prepare

1 Cream fresh yeast with 3 tbsp measured liquid in which the sugar has been dissolved. Dried yeast should be mixed with one-third of the measured liquid with sugar dissolved in it, whisked and allowed to stand in a warm room for 10-15 minutes until frothy.

2 Pour the wholewheat flour into a bowl, sieve the white flour and salt on top and mix well.

3 Make a well in the centre of the flour, pour in the oil, and cover with flour. Add the yeast mixture and most of the liquid. Mix well until dough leaves the side of the bowl, adding the remaining liquid if mixture is too dry. You may need a little extra liquid to take up the wholewheat flour but do not add too much.

4 Turn onto a floured board and knead well until a smooth elastic dough is made after about 10 minutes.

5 Put back into the bowl and cover with plastic wrap or place the dough in an oiled plastic bag. Allow to rise in a warm kitchen until doubled in size, this will take 45 minutes to an hour. Knock back (punch down) the dough and shape as required.

Makes 2 × 30-cm (12-in) or 3 × 20-cm (8-in) pizzas

PIZZAS

Deep dish mozzarella and salami pizza

DEEP DISH MOZZARELLA AND SALAMI PIZZA

Ingredients
2¼ cups/225 g/8 oz flour made into pizza dough (page 102)
Topping
1½ cups/425 g/15 oz canned tomatoes, drained
2 tsp oil
1 tsp origanum
12 slices Italian salami
12 thin slices mozzarella cheese
2 tbsp parmesan cheese
salt and freshly ground pepper
½ cup/50 g/2 oz black olives
Oven temperature 220°C/425°F/Gas 7

To prepare

1 Make the dough and allow to rise. Knock back and shape in 2 ×20-cm (8-in) flan rings (pie plates) placed on a baking sheet or sandwich cake pans.

2 Mash down the tomatoes and add a little of the drained juice.

3 Brush the dough with oil and arrange the tomatoes on the bottom.

4 Roll the salami into rounds. Sprinkle a little parmesan cheese on the tomato and then the origanum. Arrange the salami rolls.

5 Place the slices of mozzarella cheese alternately with salami. Season well.

6 Sprinkle on the remaining Parmesan and decorate the whole with black olives.

7 Brush over with oil and cook in a hot oven for 20 minutes. Reduce the heat to 190°C/375°F/Gas 5 for a further 5-10 minutes.

Makes 2 × 20-cm (8-in) pizzas

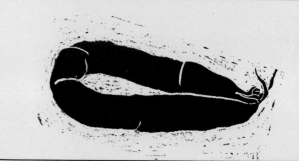

PIZZAS

DEEP DISH HAM AND MUSHROOM PIZZA

Ingredients

2¼ cups/225 g/8 oz flour made into pizza dough (page 102)

1 tbsp oil

1¼ cups/300 ml/½ pt well flavoured bechamel sauce

salt and freshly ground pepper

1½ cups/425 g/15 oz canned tomatoes, drained

½ tsp origanum

6 slices of cooked ham

2 cups/100 g/4 oz mushrooms, washed and sliced

1 cup/100 g/4 oz mozzarella cheese, thinly sliced

Oven temperature 210°C/425°F/Gas 7

To prepare

1 Shape the risen dough.

2 Brush over the dough with oil and divide the bechamel sauce between the two bases.

3 Arrange half the sliced mushrooms on the bechamel sauce.

4 Chop the canned tomatoes and divide between the two bases. Season well and sprinkle with origanum.

5 Cut the slices of ham in two and roll them up, placing 6 rolls on each pizza alternating with thin slices of mozzarella cheese. Garnish with sliced mushrooms.

6 Bake in a hot oven for 15 minutes and then reduce the heat to 190°C/375°F/Gas 5 for a further 10 minutes.

These pizzas make a very substantial meal; two of them should serve four average appetites.

Makes 2 × 20-cm (8-in) pizzas

DEEP DISH ARTICHOKE HEART AND BACON PIZZA

Ingredients
2¼ cups/225 g/8 oz flour made into pizza dough (page 102)
1 tbsp olive oil
1¼ cups/300 ml/½ pt pomodoro sauce (page 43)
1 can artichoke hearts
12 slices bacon
1 tbsp parmesan cheese
1 tbsp freshly chopped basil or parsley leaves
Oven temperature 210°C/425°F/Gas 7

To prepare

1 Shape the risen dough as shown on page 101 into flan rings (pie plates) or sandwich cake pans (tins).

2 Brush over the dough with the oil and divide the pomodoro sauce between the two bases.

3 Drain the artichoke hearts.

4 Roll up the slices of bacon and cook under the grill (broiler) or in the oven for a few minutes.

5 Sprinkle the pizzas with parmesan cheese and herbs.

6 Arrange the artichoke hearts alternately with the bacon rolls. Brush over with the remaining oil.

7 Cook in a hot oven for 15-20 before reducing the heat to medium (190°C/375°F/Gas 5) for a further 5 minutes.

Makes 2 × 20-cm (8-in) pizzas

NEAPOLITAN PIZZA

Ingredients
2¼ cups/225 g/8 oz flour made into pizza dough (page 102)
1 tbsp olive oil
1 clove garlic, crushed
6 tomatoes, skinned and sliced
½ tsp origanum
4 chopped basil leaves
Oven temperature 220°C/450°F/Gas 7-8

To prepare

1 Take the 2¼ cups/225 g/8 oz portion of dough and roll into a round shape, kneading the round out to the large 30-cm (12-in) size with floured knuckles. Make sure that it is not too thick. Any left-over dough can be allowed to rise and cooked as a bread roll.

A large flan tin (pie plate) is ideal for this type of pizza but it shapes well on a greased baking tray.

2 Brush over the dough with the olive oil and rub over the whole surface with the well crushed clove of garlic.

3 Arrange the tomatoes over the surface and sprinkle with herbs. Fresh parsley may be used if basil is unobtainable. Season well.

4 Place in a hot oven for 20-25 minutes.

This is the basic tomato pizza but most people prefer to add extra ingredients.

Makes 1 × 30-cm (12-in) pizza

TOMATO AND GREEN OLIVE PIZZA

Make as above but add ⅓ cup/50 g/2 oz grated parmesan cheese and ¼ cup/25 g/1 oz stoned green olives.

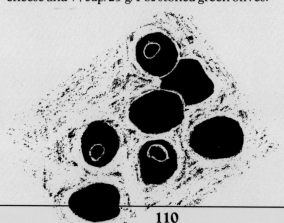

DEEP DISH MUSHROOM AND PROSCIUTTO PIZZA

Ingredients
2¼ cups/225 g/8 oz wholewheat flour made into dough (page 103)
Topping
1 tbsp oil
1½ cups/425 g/15 oz canned tomatoes, drained
4 tomatoes, skinned and peeled
1 tsp origanum
2 tbsp parmesan cheese
6 cups/350 g/12 oz mushrooms, washed and sliced
8 slices thin smoked ham (prosciutto)
salt and freshly ground pepper
Oven temperature 220°C/425°F/Gas 7

To prepare

1 Shape the dough as for deep dish pizza.

2 Paint the shaped dough with a pastry brush dipped in oil.

3 Arrange the tomatoes on the bases of the pizza dough. Sprinkle with origanum and salt and pepper.

4 Sprinkle half the cheese over the tomato mixture.

5 Melt the butter and the remaining oil in a frying pan and allow the mushrooms to cook over a low heat for about 4 minutes.

6 Spread the mushrooms on top of the pizzas and arrange the ham on top. Sprinkle with the remaining cheese.

7 Cook in a hot oven for 15 minutes, before turning the oven down to 190°C/375°F/Gas 5 for the last 10 minutes.

Makes 2 × 20-cm (8-in) pizzas

FOUR CHEESE PIZZA

Make the Neapolitan pizza but substitute 4 different cheeses for parmesan. This pizza has ¼ cup/25 g/1 oz each of mozzarella cheese, gruyere cheese, blue cheese and grated cheddar. It is an excellent way to use up small pieces of cheese.

Four cheese pizza

PIZZAS

WHOLEWHEAT PEPPER AND CAPER PIZZA

Ingredients

2¼ cups/225 g/8 oz wholewheat flour made into pizza (page 102)

1 tbsp oil

1½ cups/425 g/15 oz canned tomatoes

½ tsp fresh or ¼ tsp dried thyme

3 cups/175 g/6 oz mushrooms, washed and sliced

1 red pepper, seeded

1 tbsp capers, chopped

salt and freshly ground pepper

2 tbsp parmesan cheese

Oven temperatures 220°C/425°F/Gas 7

To prepare

1 Shape the dough into 2 × 20-cm (8-in) pizzas and brush with oil.

2 Drain and chop the tomatoes, mix with the thyme and spread on the pizza bases. Arrange the mushrooms on the two bases and sprinkle with chopped capers. Season well.

3 Sprinkle with grated cheese and arrange strips of red pepper on top. Bake for 15 minutes in a hot oven and then reduce the temperature to 190°C/375°F/Gas 5 for another 10 minutes.

Makes 2 × 20-cm (8-in) pizzas

PIZZA SICILIANA

Ingredients
2¼ cups/225 g/8 oz flour made into risen pizza dough
⅝ cup/150 ml/¼ pt tomato sauce (page 42)
4 tomatoes, skinned and sliced
½ tsp oregano
salt and freshly ground pepper
⅓ cup/50 g/2 oz parmesan cheese
1 can anchovies
good ½ cup/75 g/ 3 oz black olives
Oven temperature 220°C/425°F/Gas 7

To prepare

1 Shape the dough into a rectangular shape 30 cm (12 in) × 20 cms (8 in) or use a flan tin (pie plate) or large swiss roll (jelly roll) pan.

2 Paint the dough with a pastry brush dipped in oil and then cover the surface with the tomato sauce.

3 Place the sliced tomatoes on top and sprinkle with oregano and seasoning.

4 Sprinkle with parmesan cheese.

5 Drain the can of anchovies and arrange the halved fillets in a lattice design. Place an olive in the centre of each lattice.

6 Paint over with the remaining oil and bake in a hot oven for 15 minutes. Then turn the heat down to 190°C/ 375°F/Gas 5 for a further 10 minutes.

Serves 2-4

Make the pizza up as for Siciliana as far as painting the dough with oil and arranging the sauce on top. Add 1 can chopped tomatoes. Dice a green pepper into small pieces, blanch it for 2 minutes and drain it. Scatter the oregano and pepper on the tomato mixture, followed by ¾ cup/75 g/3 oz grated cheddar. Cut 3 pork sausages in pieces diagonally and arrange on the top of the pizza. Cook as described opposite.

WHOLEWHEAT AUBERGINE (EGGPLANT) & MOZZARELLA PIZZA

Ingredients

1 cup/100 g/4 oz flour made into wholewheat pizza dough
2 tbsp oil
1 small aubergine (eggplant), sliced
salt and freshly ground pepper
⅝ cup/150 ml/¼ pt tomato sauce (page 42)
1 small red pepper, seeded
3 stuffed olives, halved
½ cup/50 g/2 oz mozzarella cheese
Oven temperature 220°C/425°F/Gas 7

To prepare

1 Shape the pizza into a 20-cm (8-in) round and rub a little oil over the dough.

2 Sprinkle the sliced aubergine with salt and allow it to stand for a few minutes.

3 Spread the tomato sauce over the dough.

4 Cut 6 rings of red pepper.

5 Heat the remaining oil in the frying pan. Drain the aubergine slices of juice on kitchen paper and fry for about 30 seconds on each side.

6 Arrange them on the pizza with a ring of red pepper on top and half an olive in the centre. Place the slices of mozzarella between the aubergine slices and cook in a hot oven for 15 minutes. Turn the heat down 190°C/375°F/Gas 5 for the final 10 minutes.

Makes 1 × 20-cm (8-in) pizza

INDIVIDUAL BLUE CHEESE PIZZA

> Use 2¼ cups/225 g/8 oz wholewheat flour made into
> dough shaped into 4 × 10-cm (4-in) flan tins (pie plates)

Rub with oil and spread ⅝ cup/150 ml/¼ pt tomato sauce
on the bottom of each. Arrange small pieces of blue
cheese in a circle round the outside — the pizzas will take
about 1 cup/100 g/4 oz cheese. Garnish with strips of
pepper and olives. Cook for 20 minutes in a hot oven.

Individual blue cheese pizza

POTATO PAN PIZZA

Ingredients
Potato Base
2¼ cups/225 g/8 oz cooked, sieved potatoes
2¼ cups/225 g/8 oz plain flour
1 tsp salt
½ level tsp dried mustard
1 tsp mixed herbs
6 tbsp/75 g/3 oz butter
1 egg, beaten
½ cup/50 g/2 oz grated cheese
⅝ cup/150 ml/¼ pt milk
⅝ cup/150 ml/¼ pt oil for frying
Topping
1 onion, peeled and chopped
1½ cups/425 g/15 oz canned tomatoes, drained
1 tsp dried basil
salt and pepper
1½ cups/175 g/6 oz grated cheese
Optional garnish
anchovies, black olives or slices of cooked ham
Oven temperature 190°C/375°F/Gas 5

To prepare

1 Mix the butter with the warm sieved potatoes in a
bowl. Weigh the potato after cooking to make sure
proportions are correct.

2 Sieve in the flour, salt, dried mustard and herbs. Mix
with the egg, add the cheese and make a stiff dough with
milk.

3 Turn onto a floured board and divide the mixture into
6. Roll into rounds approximately 12 cm (5 in) in
diameter.

4 Heat the oil in a deep frying pan and fry the potato
bases until golden brown each side.

5 Arrange on a baking sheet and prepare the filling.

6 Drain the frying pan and clean out with some kitchen
paper. Pour back a little of the strained oil and cook the
finely chopped onion for 4 minutes over a low heat, add
the canned tomatoes and break up in the pan. Season well
and mix in the basil.

7 Divide the tomato filling between the potato bases and
cover them with cheese. Any other topping can be added
at this stage.

8 Cook for 10 minutes or until golden brown in the
preheated oven.

Serves 6

TUNA SCONE PIZZA

Ingredients
2¼ cups/225 g/8 oz flour made into scone dough (page 124)
Topping
1 tsp oil
1½ cups/450 g/1 lb tomatoes, skinned and sliced
1 cup/100 g/4 oz cheddar cheese
scant 1 cup/200 g/7 oz canned tuna fish
½ tsp mixed herbs
salt and pepper
7 black olives
Oven temperature 210°C/425°F/Gas 7

To prepare

1 Make the scone mixture and roll out to a 25-cm (10-in) round.

2 Paint over with oil and arrange the sliced tomatoes. Sprinkle with half the cheese.

3 Arrange the tuna fish evenly around the outside of the pizza and sprinkle all over with mixed herbs. Season well.

4 Finish with a layer of cheese. Arrange the olives in a ring near the centre of the circle.

5 Paint over with oil and cook in a preheated hot oven. Turn the oven down after 10 minutes to 190°C/375°F/Gas 5 for the remaining 15-20 minutes cooking time.

6 Serve immediately.

Serves 2-4

QUICK SUPPER PIZZA

Ingredients
2¼ cups/225 g/8 oz self-raising flour
½ level tsp salt
1 level tsp baking powder
½ level tsp dried mustard
4 tbsp/50 g/2 oz butter
⅝ cup/150 ml/¼ pt milk
Topping
1½ cups/450 g/1 lb tomatoes, peeled and sliced
½ tsp origanum or basil
2 cups/225 g/8 oz cheddar cheese
salt and pepper
8 anchovy fillets
12 black olives
1 tsp oil
Oven temperature 220°C/450°F/Gas 7

To prepare

1 Sieve the flour and salt into a mixing bowl.

2 Cut the butter into small pieces and rub into the flour with the tips of the fingers until the mixture resembles fine breadcrumbs.

3 Add most of the milk and mix to a soft dough. Add the remaining milk unless it will make the dough too sticky.

4 Roll out the dough into a 25-cm (10-in) circle, keeping the shape as round as possible. The bottom of a cake pan can be used as a guide.

5 Sprinkle a little cheese on the scone round, then some slices of tomato with a sprinkling of origanum or basil and a shake of salt and pepper. Sprinkle more cheese on the round, then add the remaining tomatoes, herbs and seasoning. Finish with a layer of grated cheese.

6 Decorate with strips of anchovy and black olives. Paint over with oil.

7 Place in a preheated oven for 8 minutes then turn the heat down to 200°C/400°F/Gas 6 for about 15 minutes until pizza is golden and cooked.
    Serve immediately.

Serves 2-4

WHOLEWHEAT SCONE PIZZA

Ingredients
1¼ cups/125 g/5 oz wholewheat flour
¾ cup/75 g/3 oz plain flour
4 level tsp baking powder
½ tsp salt
3 tbsp/40 g/1½ oz butter
⅝ cup/150 ml/¼ pt milk

Topping
2 tbsp oil
1 onion, peeled and diced
1 pepper, seeded
2 cups/100 g/4 oz mushrooms, washed and sliced
½ cup/50 g/2 oz grated cheese
4 tomatoes, peeled and sliced
1 tsp fresh mixed herbs
Oven temperature 220°C/425°F/Gas 7

To prepare

1 Pour the wholewheat flour into a mixing bowl, sieve the white flour, baking powder and salt into the bowl and mix well.

2 Rub in the butter with the tips of the fingers until the mixture resembles fine breadcrumbs.

3 Add the milk and mix to a soft dough, a further small quantity of milk may be needed to mix the dough to the correct consistency. Turn on to a lightly floured board and knead lightly into a round shape.

4 Roll out into a 25-cm (10-in) round and place on a baking sheet.

5 To start the filling, heat the oil in a frying pan and cook the onions over a low heat for 4 minutes.

6 Cut the pepper into thin rings and blanch in boiling water for 2 minutes. Drain.

7 Add the washed, sliced mushrooms to the onion and allow to cook for a further 2 minutes.

8 Arrange the tomatoes on the scone base and sprinkle with mixed herbs and seasoning.

9 Arrange mushrooms and onions on top of the tomatoes, and sprinkle with cheese. Put the rings of peppers on last.

10 Cook in a preheated oven for 10 minutes reducing the heat to 190°C/375°F/Gas 5 for a further 10 minutes.

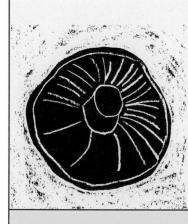